"Michael's work has saved my butt on more than one occasion — and I keep having occasions, so I'm glad he's still at work. If you want to be a better writer, and a better presenter of your own work, stop reading this quote and go buy the book!"

— Jeff Arch, Screenwriter: *Sleepless in Seattle*; *Iron Will*; *Saving Milly*; Writer/Director: *Dave Barry's Complete Guide to Guys*

"Finally, someone's got it right. Michael Hauge's book is insightful and totally on the mark for anyone interested in pitching their screenplay. Write a screenplay, then read this book, and half the work is done."

— Syd Field, Screenwriter, Lecturer, Author: *Screenplay*; *The Screenwriter's Workbook*; *The Screenwriter's Problem Solver*

"Please! You must buy this book!!"

— Vicki Arthur, wife of Michael Hauge

"Michael Hauge has done it again! First he taught us how to write a great screenplay, now we know how to get it sold. This book is insightful, fun to read, and so inspiring you'll be dying to pitch something the moment you put it down. If you're serious about a career in screenwriting, read this book immediately."

— Jon Gunn, Writer/Director: *My Date with Drew*; *Mercy Streets*

"For 25 years I have been telling UCLA graduate screenwriting students, 'You sell in the first minute! From then on it's filler.' Well, Michael Hauge shows rather than tells how in this terrific book."

— Lew Hunter, UCLA Dept. of Film and TV; Producer/Screenwriter: *Fallen Angel*; *Playing with Fire*; Author: *Screenwriting 434*; *Naked Screenwriting: Interviews with 20 Academy Award-Winning Directors and Writers*

"Props to Michael Hauge, who once again advances his timeless insights, this time into perhaps the most under-utilized tool in the professional writer's war chest: the telephone pitch. Armed with his savvy methods, you'll commandeer the meaningful consideration you and your work deserve."

— Diane Cairns, Producer, Screenwriter; former Senior VP, ICM; former Senior VP of Production, Universal Pictures

"Every writer on the planet — at any level of their craft — can benefit from what Michael Hauge has to say about pitching. He knows — and knows how to explain — the secret handshakes that can get you inside the tight little circle of working writers. Read this book and then read it again!"

— Catherine Clinch, Associate Publisher, *Creative Screenwriting Magazine*

"Give Hauge a minute; he'll give you a career. This book is so full of insights and practical help that we've made it an official selection of the Great American PitchFest."

— Signe Olynyk, President/CEO, Great American PitchFest

"Do yourself a favor and memorize this book! Michael Hauge delivers the core strategies of getting agents, producers and studio execs to spend their most valuable asset — their time — on your hard work."

— John Johnson, Executive Director, American Screenwriters Association

"Michael Hauge dares to use the word 'Guaranteed' in his subtitle and then delivers the information that justifies it. If you can't get your novel or screenplay in front of the editor or agent you most want to read it, you aren't following his instructions."

— Alfie Thompson, Author: *Lights! Camera! Fiction! A Movie Lover's Guide to Writing a Novel*

"Finally comes a book that addresses one of the most important, and ignored, aspects of selling screen stories and novels. When you finally get to sit down with a producer, agent or editor, the way you tell them about your story can make the difference between a sale and a rejection, and between a smaller payout and a large one. Read this book."

— Bob Reiss, Author: *The Side Effect, The Last Spy, Dead for Life*

"I wish I had read this book before Warner Brothers nixed the last idea I tried to sell them. How was I supposed to know that Hollywood does not like comedies about cheese?"

— Patty Marx, former Staff Writer: *Saturday Night Live*; Author: *Him Her Him Again The End of Him*

"Michael Hauge gives you everything you need to get your material noticed and read by those with the power to give you a career in return. It's all about being prepared, and with this book, you will be ready to pitch your project professionally and passionately wherever and whenever you need to."

— Marie Jones, *Bookideas.com, AbsoluteWrite.com*

"Mastering the 60-second pitch is an art and craft in itself, and regardless of what you're pitching — screenplay, book, concept or finished film — potential buyers must be captivated by the story and emotional power you convey with clarity and brevity. Hauge is at his coaching best as he focuses on the process of optimizing resources to make the most of those golden opportunities."

— Maureen Herzog, Editor/Co-Publisher: *Indie Slate Magazine*

"This is an amazing book that really puts the nuts and bolts of the 60-second pitch in your hands. He devotes nearly 40 pages of a 180-page book to executives from all over the Hollywood food chain, to explain what works and doesn't work during a pitch. A MUST for anyone with an idea to sell. Thank God for this book."

— Matthew Terry, *Hollywoodlitsales.com*

"Concise, direct, and to the point. Don't make another pitch until you have read this book."

— Anne Marie Gillen, CEO/Founder, Gillen Group, LLC; Cabin 14 Productions; Producer: *Under Suspicion, Fried Green Tomatoes*

"I won first place in the Pitch Slam competition just by using the techniques I learned from Michael Hauge. They put me in control of the meeting, I was able to relax, and they really worked! And I know it was his system, because I've used this pitch before. But this time, it sold!"

— Rosa Graham, Screenwriter; Founder of *Find the Funny*

"In this wonderful book, Michael Hauge covers all the bases, and turns the 'simple, but not easy' task of pitching into something you can do with genuine confidence. Honestly, with these tools you may even find pitching fun!"

— Ellen Sandler, Screenwriter, Co-Executive Producer: *Everybody Loves Raymond*; Author: *The TV Writer's Workbook: A Creative Approach to Television Scripts*

"Before you go to a writer's conference or a pitch fest or a meeting in Hollywood, you must read this book. In fact, before you write your next script, peruse these pages filled with wit and wisdom from one of the only writing gurus in town who really knows his stuff. Get out your wallet. Go to the counter. Buy this freaking book!"

— Rich Krevolin, Author: *Screenwriting from the Soul*; *How to Adapt Anything into a Screenplay*

"Anyone trying to master the art of pitching needs this invaluable resource taught by the master himself. Michael Hauge has opened his heart (and his veins) and poured his hard-earned secrets into accessible tips and a must-have guide for anyone trying to sell their script or get their book published."

— Devorah Cutler-Rubenstein, CEO, The Script Broker; Author: *What's the Big Idea? Writing Award-Winning Shorts*

"One of the hottest, most cogent books about pitching, selling and marketing stories I have read. It's all here. All you have to do is read it, pick up the phone and make the call, take the meeting, do the deal. Simple, sensible advice for everyone trying to sell a story."

— Jeff Freedman, Screenwriter/Consulting Producer: *Vivaldi*

"If you are serious about your writing, invest in yourself and your career — buy this book and acquaint yourself with Michael Hauge's caveats on designing, practicing and presenting your projects. It's worth every penny and then some!"

— Kathie Fong Yoneda, Seminar Leader, Executive Producer: *Beyond the Break*; Author: *The Script-Selling Game: A Hollywood Insider's Look at Getting Your Script Sold and Produced*

"I was fortunate enough to work with Michael on one of my projects. He has a remarkable ability not only to detect the weaknesses in a script, but to suggest solutions. He is also incredibly fun to work with — his creativity is infectious!"

— Kerry David, Producer: *Agent Cody Banks*; *My Date with Drew*; *Perfect Romance*

"Michael Hauge is my secret weapon for creating stories that sell in today's super-competitive market. I wouldn't dream of pitching a story without first booking a few hours with Michael to get his laser-sharp feedback."

— Paul Margolis, Screenwriter: *John Carpenter's The 13th Apostle*; *Ticker*; Writer/Producer: *Pacific Blue*; *Sirens*; *MacGyver*

"I've known Michael for more than ten years, and from my experience he's the best script consultant in the business."

— Paul S. Levine, Entertainment Attorney, Literary Agent

"In a field choked with alleged 'script doctors,' Michael Hauge remains the surest, most sensible alternative. When I pick up the phone for help, he's the call I make."
— Shane Black, Screenwriter: *Lethal Weapon 1 & 2*; *The Last Boy Scout*; *The Long Kiss Goodnight*; Screenwriter/Director: *Kiss Kiss Bang Bang*

"The only screenwriting instructor out there who might be truly wasting his time — because he should be writing screenplays instead. Higher praise I cannot give."
— Terry Rossio, Screenwriter (with Ted Elliott): *Pirates of the Caribbean 1, 2 & 3*; *Shrek*; *Aladdin*; *The Mask of Zorro*; (with Bill Marsilli): *Deja Vu*

"My writing partner and I have made most of our sales — including *Wedding Crashers* — by pitching. Over the years, through trial and error, stumbling, stuttering, and a fair amount of humiliation, we've become pretty good at it. I wish this excellent book had been around when we were starting out — it would have saved me most of the humiliation, and some of the stuttering."
— Bob Fisher, Screenwriter (with Steve Faber): *Wedding Crashers*; *We're the Millers*

"A wonderful book — important, accessible and user-friendly. Michael knows just what's needed to get that script through that difficult Hollywood door. He makes the impossible look possible, and the possible look accessible. An absolute MUST for every screenwriter who wants to sell a script."
— Dr. Linda Seger, Script Consultant, Seminar Leader, Author, *Making a Good Script Great*; *Advanced Screenwriting*

"Once again, Michael Hauge has done the heavy lifting for screenwriters and novelists. Drawn from his years of nursing projects through the system to production and publication, this book distills everything you need to know about packaging and presenting your stories to the people who can say yes. Your chances of getting them to say that magic word will definitely be improved by readying and applying the know-how in this book."
— Christopher Vogler, Story Analyst, Paramount Pictures; Author: *The Writer's Journey: Mythic Structure for Writers*

"I feel very lucky to have met Michael Hauge in my quest to become a better writer — he offers a winning combination of encouragement and insight, bolstered by deep and informed understanding of the art of storytelling. This is much more than a book about sales — it's a book about telling good stories, and turning your dreams into reality."
— Shelley Evans, Screenwriter: *One Kill* (Showtime); *Footsteps* (CBS); *A Girl Like Me* (Lifetime)

"*Selling Your Story in 60 Seconds* is filled with solid gold nuggets. If you can enunciate your essence and intrigue your audience in the way Michael Hauge describes, you have a blockbuster in the making."
— Linda Bauer, Columnist, Lecturer, Author: *The American Sampler Cookbook* series

SELLING

YOUR STORY IN

60 SECONDS

THE GUARANTEED WAY TO GET
YOUR SCREENPLAY OR NOVEL READ

MICHAEL HAUGE

Published by Michael Wiese Productions
3940 Laurel Canyon Blvd. Suite 1111
Studio City, CA 91604
tel. 818.379.8799
fax 818.986.3408
mw@mwp.com
www.mwp.com

Cover Design: MWP
Book Layout: Gina Mansfield
Editor: Paul Norlen
Author Photo: © 2006 Jody Frank

Printed by McNaughton & Gunn, Inc., Saline, Michigan
Manufactured in the United States of America

© 2006 Michael Hauge

Library of Congress Cataloging-in-Publication Data

Hauge, Michael.
 Selling your story in 60 seconds : the guaranteed way to get your screenplay or novel read / Michael Hauge.
     p. cm.
 ISBN 1-932907-20-3
1. Motion picture authorship--Marketing. 2. Fiction--Marketing. I. Title. II. Title: Selling your story in sixty seconds.
PN1996.H358 2006
808.2'3--dc22

                                        2006023974

To my wonderful brother
Jim Hauge
who loves movies as much as I do

CONTENTS

PART II: PRESENTATION

PART III: EXTRA STUFF

ACKNOWLEDGMENTS

As I was in the process of completing this book, this year's Academy Awards ceremony was held, and I realized how much an acknowledgments page is like an Oscar speech. You're trying to thank everyone who contributed to the work you did. But then you think, "*Well, if I thank them, I better thank these other people, too, or they'll think they don't mean as much to me.*" And pretty soon you're just worried about who you might forget to mention.

At least I have more than two minutes, or whatever absurd amount of time the Academy gives the winners. Not the *stars,* of course; they can prattle on as long as they want. But it's all the time the lowly screenwriters ever get, before that awful orchestra starts to play them off.

So I want to thank, certainly, the people that truly helped bring this book to completion. But even more than that, I want to thank some people whose contributions to my career, or to my life, make what I do — including writing this book — so rewarding, and so much fun.

Starting with my assistant, Ginger Earle, who did research, and transcribing, and whatever else I needed day after day. She was the first person to read the manuscript of this book, and she did what only the best editors do — she told me when something excited her or made her laugh, not just what didn't work.

Huge thanks, of course, to Michael Wiese and Ken Lee at Michael Wiese Productions, who took a big chance when they agreed to publish this book, based only on my assurances that it was a good idea. From the moment I contacted them, they've made me feel welcome and special. And to my editor, Paul Norlen, and to Gina Mansfield, who created the book's layout, thanks for making the words flow and the pages look great.

Thanks to Esther Newberg, my terrific agent at ICM, and to her assistant, Christine Earle, who is always helpful and supportive, even with all my panicky calls asking why lawyers take so long getting contracts written.

To all the generous writers and agents and executives in Chapter 12, who offered their comments and suggestions about pitching, thank you from a very grateful author, and from all of the readers who will be enlightened and empowered by your insights. And to my clients and associates and friends as well, who provided all those back- and inside-cover quotes that make me sound way smarter and more special than I really am.

Again and again I feel deeply appreciated and honored by the sponsors and organizations who invite me to speak, especially John Johnson and the American Screenwriters Association; Erik Bauer and the Screenwriting EXPO; and Derek Christopher and TV/Film Seminars and Workshops. And without the wisdom, trust and commitment of my consulting clients and seminar participants, I simply wouldn't have anything to say in this book — or any desire to say it. I'm one of the lucky, lucky few in this world who get to make a living doing what they love. It's all of you I have to thank for that.

And without playing favorites, I have to add a special acknowledgment to six terrific writers and filmmakers I've been working with — and friends with — for a long, rewarding time: Grace Boyett; Diane Cairns; Robert Celestino; Teresa Cutler; Heather Hale; and Roger Stone. Thanks, and hang in there — we're all gonna be rich soon.

Most of the people I'm about to mention were also acknowledged in my previous book. Since that was written more than fifteen years ago, you can see how blessed I've been to have these people in my life. So continued love and thanks to my brother Jim and his new bride Jennifer (who likes movies as long as they aren't violent or gross or scary or upsetting); and to Bruce Derman, Eric Edson, Dianne Haak, Mitchell Group and Paul Margolis, not only for your treasured friendship, but for years of great conversations about movies.

And deep appreciation to Cisci Deschaine, Heidi Wall Roberts, Donna Jason, Justine Dantzer, John Lofgren, and Nancy Lynn Newman (who I have to include just so I can spell her name right this time), who almost never talk about movies, but with whom I can talk about anything else, and who are always there with love and support and laughter.

As always, thanks to my friends in Oregon, Charles Moreland, Jim and Nancy Hicks, John and Teresa Hudkins, and Bill and Wendy Trezise. I was dragging those four guys to movies at the Elsinore Theater all the way back in the seventh grade (which, if anyone in Hollywood asks, was about fifteen years ago). They've been my best friends ever since.

Finally, and most of all, love and thanks to my wife Vicki, who never stops believing in me, never stops encouraging me to write, and who is still my favorite person in the world to sneak away with on a Friday afternoon to see a movie.

INTRODUCTION

Selling a screenplay or a novel is simple. It's not easy, but it's simple.

Step number one: *Write a great story*.

Step number two: *Get lots and lots of people to read it*.

My previous book, *Writing Screenplays That Sell*, as well as hundreds of lectures, dozens of articles, a bunch of CDs and DVDs, and thousands of hours I've spent coaching writers and filmmakers, have mostly been about step one.

This book is about step two.

You can have the greatest, most commercial, most brilliantly written screenplay or manuscript since *The Godfather*, but if you don't get dozens of agents, managers, producers, editors and executives in the film or publishing industries to read it, it'll never get produced, and you'll never reach the wide audience you long for.

So how do you do that? How do you somehow persuade all those powerful people that your work is worth their time? That it is more likely to make them money, or fulfill their passion for storytelling, than the scores of other scripts and book proposals they already have to read? And how do you accomplish this seemingly impossible task when you have at best only a minute or two of their time before they hang up, turn away or move on to the next hopeful writer knocking on their door?

The 60-Second Pitch

This book is about selling. But despite the catchy title, it's not really about selling your screenplay or novel. It's about selling someone the *opportunity* to read your story. This book will teach you how to convince potential agents and buyers to spend their most valuable asset — their time — in exchange for the personal and financial riches your story will bring.

In other words, this book is about a certain kind of sales pitch, what I term the *60-second pitch* — sometimes known as the *telephone pitch*, or the *elevator pitch*, or the *pitch fest pitch*. Because it's a pitch you have less than two minutes to deliver.

A 60-second pitch should not to be confused with a pitch *meeting*. In a pitch meeting, a writer (usually a screenwriter; pitch meetings are rare in the publishing world) has been invited to come to an agent or executive's office and outline a story in detail. The meeting can last from 15 to 45 minutes or more, and often includes a whole conference table full of people. The writer's goal is usually to secure a development deal, and to get paid for turning a story into a complete screenplay.

Pitch meetings and development deals usually occur after a writer's career is established, or at least after the person receiving the pitch has read other samples of the writer's work, or is familiar with what the writer has had produced or published. For that to have happened, the writer must have persuaded lots of people to read her earlier work. And she did that by using some form of the 60-second pitch.

I'll discuss pitch meetings in some detail in Chapter 10, and reveal how the techniques of the 60-second pitch can be applied to a longer presentation. But if you're a writer still trying to launch your career — still looking for representation or a first option or sale — the opportunities for pitch meetings will be pretty rare. The opportunities that demand that you master the 60-second pitch, however, will form the backbone of your entire marketing campaign.

If you're not a novelist or screenwriter, but are a reader, assistant or intern hoping to move up the ladder to become an agent, development executive, editor or producer, the ability to pitch a story quickly, concisely and powerfully will do more to advance your career than almost any other skill you can master.

The Cardinal Rule of Pitching

If you're standing in the aisle at Barnes and Noble or Borders, or if you're reading this page on Amazon.com (where they let you look at a few pages to lure you into placing an order), I'm going to give you the most important principle of the entire book right now, for free. You don't even have to buy the book.

Without question, the single biggest mistake writers make in pitching their work is this: *They try to tell their story.*

Let's say you've signed up for the Pitch Xchange at the Screenwriting EXPO, or for a one-on-one session with an agent at a writers conference or book fair.

You've got maybe five minutes sitting across from this buyer to get him to look at your book or screenplay. So talking as fast as you can, you launch into the opening scene, then go on to detail, step by step, the plot of your story.

Here's what's going to happen. You'll barely be into Act 2 (or Chapter 2) when the friendly hall monitor will come over to announce that you have 30 seconds left. So you'll quickly try to penetrate the glazed expression on the buyer's face, summarize the ending, and get him to say yes.

He won't.

If you've got a story that can be told in five minutes, you've got a story for a five-minute movie. There's simply no way you can do justice to the plot of a novel or feature film in that amount of time. And even if you could, you've left no time for the buyer to react to your story by asking questions or giving suggestions or expressing his interest.

Or let's say you've managed to get a potential agent on the phone, and she's willing to hear your pitch. Literary agents have phone lists that average *at least a hundred calls a day*. They simply don't have time to listen to you detail all the elements of your story. They want to know in an instant if this story will be worth their time (or more accurately, worth the time of the reader they'll pay to do coverage on it).

So what *can* you do if you don't tell her your story?

Simply put, you get her to read your screenplay or manuscript by getting her to feel something positive about it.

The Primary Objective of All Story

The goal of every screenplay, every movie, every novel, every story of any kind (and ultimately, every work of art) is identical: *to elicit emotion.*

We go to the movies and we read books so we can *feel* something positive or fulfilling, something we can't feel as frequently or as intensely in our everyday lives. The storyteller's job is to create that feeling for the mass audience.

When you're pitching your story, you must provide buyers with a positive emotional experience. And you must convince them that when your movie is made, or your novel is published or your play is produced, your story will create an even stronger emotional experience for the people who buy tickets and books and DVDs.

In other words, your goal is to get your buyers to think, "This is a novel (or movie) I'd like to see," or more important, "*This is a story that will make a lot of money.*"

Like it or not, the 60-second pitch is a *sales* pitch. Even though the immediate goal is just to get your story read, you're ultimately asking every potential buyer to invest her time and money representing or producing or publishing your story. The only way you'll get her to do that is if she believes the end result will be a big profit.

Even if you're pitching to agents or executives or assistants whose own money isn't on the line, these people know that they (or their bosses) will have to convince dozens of other powerful people that this story will make a bundle. If they don't consistently do that with the projects they take on, they're out of business. A telephone pitch is very much like a TV ad for a movie that's about to open, or for an upcoming TV episode. A 30-second TV spot doesn't try to show every scene or character or plot element — that would be impossible. But it will reveal something funny or sexy or suspenseful from the film, in order to convince viewers watching the commercial that the movie or TV show itself will be a wonderful emotional experience.

So this book is about getting people to feel positive enough about your story that they'll want to read it. It's about selecting the elements of the story that will excite potential buyers, and making them *eager* to get their hands on your work before anybody else does. And it's about pre-senting those key elements to the right people, in a manner so compelling that they can't say no.

The 8 Steps to a Powerful Pitch

Selling your work requires both preparation and courage. But as you will learn, the better your preparation, the less courage you'll be required to muster. If you go through the entire process I present in this book, I promise you'll not only get your stories read, you'll be far less intimidated by the prospect of pitching them.

If you're a writer or filmmaker who wants to connect with an audience, who wants to touch as many people as you can with your work, you must devote time and energy to the marketing process, just as you do to your craft. You can't remain the shy, withdrawn, introverted artist you'd probably like to be (which is why you become a writer in the first place). You've got to get your work read, which means you've got to put yourself out there in a positive, committed way and make people aware of your talent.

There are eight critical steps to creating and presenting a pitch guaranteed to get your work read. So here they are — *The 8 R's of Pitching:*

1. **Review**. You must examine your story to determine its most powerful elements – the qualities you'll reveal in your pitch. You'll then find other films or novels similar in genre, tone or demographic to substantiate the commercial potential of your own story.

2. **Write**. (Okay, I know it doesn't begin with an R, but it *sounds* like it does.) After selecting the key elements to include in your pitch, you must prepare a script of exactly what you're going to say. You won't follow it word for word — this would remove the spontaneity and flexibility you'll need — but you'll use it as a well thought-out blueprint for your presentation.

3. **Rehearse**. You must practice and practice your pitch, then rewrite it and practice it some more. You have to know your pitch so well that it becomes natural and conversational.

4. **Research**. While you're completing your screenplay or novel and preparing your pitch, you'll also be targeting your market. Using directories, reviews, interviews, websites, pitch fest lists and your own contacts, you will compile a list of the specific buyers — <u>agents,</u> editors, <u>producers</u> or publishers — that you're going to pursue. Then you'll use a variety of methods to persuade them to hear your pitch.

5. **Rapport**. As soon as you contact or meet a buyer, you must establish a personal relationship — before you begin talking about your story.

6. **Revelation**. When you finally launch your pitch, you must reveal the strongest, most emotionally involving

information about yourself and your project you can, in order to convince the buyer that it's worth reading.

7. **Request.** Once you've outlined your story, you have to ask the buyer to read it.

8. **Response.** An effective pitch means listening, not just talking. You must respond to the buyer's comments, questions and requests, both to increase his interest and to strengthen your relationship with him.

The first four steps are your **Preparation** — Part I of this book. These occur before you make your phone call or begin your pitch session.

Part II will then guide you through your **Presentation** — the four remaining steps of your pitch. I'll also show how the principles of the 60-second pitch apply to other situations: full pitch meetings; encounters where you have to pitch your story in just one or two sentences; meetings where you're pitching someone else's story as a development executive or an independent producer; or jobs requiring you to write coverage for screenplays or manuscripts.

Part III will offer some added goodies: pitching templates (scripted pitches for various genres or markets, which you can modify to suit a specific project), and finally, some wonderful contributions from more than 40 successful writers, agents, attorneys, producers, editors, development executives, and publishers on what they consider to be the qualities of great (and not-so-great) pitches.

Caveats, Disclaimers, and Excuses
Finally, a couple things I should explain or warn you about before we get into the good stuff:

- This book is about pitching stories in any form applicable: screenplays; novels; plays; short films; feature films looking for distribution; radio plays; school plays and operas. But instead of repeatedly saying "screenplays or novels, or book proposals or manuscripts," I'm going to consider all those terms interchangeable. And when I say "story," I mean a story in its written form, not just the verbalized plot of your novel or screenplay.

So if you're a novelist and you read, "Pitching your screenplay to a producer isn't as hard as it sounds," translate that to mean, "Pitching your manuscript to a publisher isn't as hard as it sounds," which also means, "Pitching your book proposal to an agent isn't as hard as it sounds."

• This brings up another issue: I will try my best to balance my references to both screenplays and novels. But I'll use more movie examples than examples from literature, because it's more likely that readers from both disciplines will have seen a particular movie than will have read a particular novel. No slight is intended, and it doesn't mean the principles don't apply equally.

Often I will use examples that are both novels *and* films, so the principle presented is true for both. And whenever there's a difference between the approaches for novelists and those for screenwriters, I'll say so. I promise.

• Similarly, "Hollywood" refers to the entire film industry, not just that scuzzy neighborhood in Los Angeles. And because there's really no comparable shorthand location for the publishing world, I'll sometimes refer to it as "New York," even though I know many wonderful publishers — including mine — are based somewhere else.

• While we're on the subject of word usage, when I say "pitch," I mean the 60-second pitch. Anything longer I'll refer to as a pitch meeting. And when I say "buyer"

I mean agent, manager, producer, editor, publisher or development executive — anyone you're trying to get to read your novel (or screenplay or book proposal).

- Continuing with the fascinating subject of syntax, this is a book for writers, and my mother was an English teacher, so I'm reluctant to include poor grammar. But repeatedly saying "he or she" or "he/she" is a pain in the ass. So I'm going to randomly mix up these pronouns; a producer will be a she, and a few paragraphs later a different producer will be a he. And if you happen to encounter a sentence that says something like, "No one wants *their* pitch to be rejected," please don't tell Mom.

- Finally, because this is a book on pitching, there isn't a lot on craft. But understanding the ten key elements of a well-written story will *greatly* strengthen your writing.

So sit back, start the process, and get ready to pitch your story. And if you're still standing in the aisle at Barnes and Noble, just go buy the book, already!

PART

I

PREPARATION

THE 10 KEY COMPONENTS
OF A COMMERCIAL STORY

T he secret of a successful 60-second pitch is to convey the most powerful elements of your story clearly, succinctly and passionately — to get the buyer emotionally involved enough that he demands to read the script.

But what are those elements? How do you decide, when you only have a minute or so, what to say, and what to leave out? And how do you abide by the cardinal rule of all telephone pitches: *Don't try to tell your story!*

Now comes the confusing part. Right out of the gate, it's going to sound like I *am* suggesting that you tell your story. Because the first step in preparing your pitch is to define all the most important elements of your screenplay or novel. Not so you can then race through them all in the hopes of grabbing your listener, but so you'll be able to choose which of these ten items will best convey the power of your story.

The choices will differ for each project. Some pitches will emphasize character, some action. Some will focus on blockbuster potential; some will rely on your personal passion. But all good pitches draw on at least three or four of these ten qualities.

So here are the ten questions you must answer about your story before you even begin to think about what you'll say during your pitch:

1. *Who is your HERO?*
Who is the protagonist who drives your story? What's the name and role (cop, teacher, college student, alien, hospital

patient, etc.) of the main character, the one the audience is rooting for through the entire story?

It's possible that your story has more than one hero — that there are two or more characters whose desires drive the plot, as in the novels *Bel Canto* and *A Long Way Down*, or the films *Wedding Crashers, Sleepless in Seattle* and *Crash*. Just make sure there's at least one.

2. Why will the reader — and audience — EMPATHIZE with your hero?

Movies, screenplays and novels are participatory events. In order to experience the emotional roller coaster they offer, audiences can't just observe the action, they must *become* the hero as she faces all the obstacles standing between her and her goal. In other words, they must empathize and identify with the hero.

To insure that your reader has this experience, you must immediately employ at least two of five key methods for establishing this psychological connection:

- **Create sympathy.** Readers identify with characters they feel sorry for, so make your hero the victim of some undeserved misfortune. Harry Potter being forced to live under the stairs by his horrific relatives in *Harry Potter and the Sorcerer's Stone*; Dewey Finn getting fired by his own band in *School of Rock*; Josey Aimes' abuse by her husband in *North Country*; Viktor Navorski being stranded in *The Terminal*; these events are all designed to get us rooting for each movie's hero.

- **Put the hero in jeopardy.** We identify with characters we worry about. *The Bourne Supremacy, Kill Bill* and all of the James Bond and Indiana Jones movies open with their heroes in life-threatening situations. And the heroes of *Bel Canto* are taken hostage by guerillas at the beginning of that novel.

This jeopardy doesn't have to involve physical danger, as long as the hero is facing the loss of something of vital importance. The possibility of Peter La Fleur losing his gym in *Dodgeball: A True Underdog Story*, or of Peter Parker losing his job and flunking out of college in *Spider-Man 2*, are equally effective at increasing our emotional ties to those heroes.

• **Make the hero likeable.** If you show your hero as kind, loving and supportive, you'll increase your reader's empathy with that character. *Elf, The Station Agent, Mean Girls, Prime,* and *Finding Nemo* all introduce us to big-hearted heroes — each one is immediately shown doing something nice for another character. And Susie Salmon, the 14-year old narrator/hero of *The Lovely Bones*, speaks lovingly about her family at the opening of the novel (plus we quickly learn that she was a murder victim, and is speaking to us from Heaven, creating sympathy for her as well).

A neat trick for exhibiting this quality in your hero is to show him as well liked by other characters in the story. *Road to Perdition* and *Munich* portray professional killers. Yet each hero is introduced as deeply loved by his family. It's only after empathy has been established that we see each one with a gun in his hand.

• **Make the hero funny.** A hero doesn't have to be lovable to be empathetic. *As Good as it Gets, Bad Santa,* and *The Bad News Bears* all portray heroes who are bigoted, insulting and generally pretty nasty. But we identify with them because they make us laugh. These are heroes we want to spend a couple hours with, and who we might even secretly admire, because they have the nerve to hurl all these mean and politically incorrect insults that we would never admit we sometimes feel.

• **Make the hero powerful.** Audiences like to root for characters who can get the job done. Not only for superheroes, but for anyone who's very good at what she does. Max's skill as a cab driver in *Collateral* serves this function, as do The Bride's fighting skills in *Kill Bill: Vol. 1* and Nathan Algren's marksmanship in *The Last Samurai*.

Notice that every successful movie or novel reveals at least two of these qualities for its hero as soon as the character is introduced. Ann Darrow in *King Kong* is sweet and kind, starving, and loses her job within ten minutes of when she's introduced. She's also a skilled vaudevillian and acrobat (a great example of *foreshadowing*, by the way, but you'll have to read my other book for an explanation of that, since it's unrelated to pitching). And we know she's in jeopardy because she's about to go meet a giant killer ape, though our anticipation of that is due more to the advertising than to the screenplay.

Empathy is something you must create *when the hero is introduced*. Making your hero a victim in the middle of the movie or showing him *becoming* kind and loving may make your story richer, but it doesn't create empathy and identification.

3. What is the SETUP of the story? Where is your hero when he's introduced, before the forward movement of the story begins? For a story to fully engage us, we must enter it before the beginning of the hero's journey. We want to see who and where the hero is before these extraordinary events begin to occur. Whether it's a young, turn-of-the-century factory worker in the novel *Specimen Days*, an author on the rise in *Capote*, a superhero in *The Incredibles*, or an electronics store employee who's secretly a *40-Year-Old Virgin*, the opening of your story must introduce us to your hero living his everyday life. It's as if you're saying to the reader, *"This is who my hero was yesterday, and for a long time before that."*

During the setup, you must create immediate empathy for your hero, using the techniques outlined in #2 above. The setup is also where you exhibit the beginning of your hero's arc. Think of it as the BEFORE side of the BEFORE AND AFTER picture you're going to reveal to the audience through the course of the story.

In the novel and film *In Her Shoes*, Maggie Feller transforms from a self-involved, thoughtless and overly dependent party girl to a woman who stands up for herself, assumes responsibility for her life and considers the needs of others. But we wouldn't appreciate the courage and growth she achieves if we hadn't seen the emotional cowardice and limited existence she exhibits at the beginning of the story.

4. What OPPORTUNITY is presented to your hero?

In a properly structured screenplay, some major event will occur 10% of the way into the story — something that will get the story into gear, and begin the hero's forward movement. In *The Ring*, Rachel learns about a mysterious videotape that might be connected to her niece's death; in *Munich*, Avner is asked to head a team of assassins; in *Million Dollar Baby*, Maggie asks Frankie to be her trainer; and in *13 Going on 30* Jenna is sprinkled with magic dust.

The 10% rule doesn't necessarily apply to novels or plays. But the need to present your hero with some opportunity early in the story, to take the plot in a new direction, is essential.

In the Nick Hornby novel *A Long Way Down*, the four heroes, intent on committing suicide, all go to the top of a well-known jump-to-your-death building on New Year's Eve. Meeting each other and being stopped from jumping is their opportunity, even though it occurs almost immediately — far sooner, relative to the length of the novel, than it would — or will — in a movie adaptation.

As a result of the opportunity, your hero will move to some new situation. When the guerillas take over the Vice President's home in the novel *Bel Canto* (the opportunity), the hostages must now figure out what's going on, and somehow survive their captivity (new situation). And in almost every Spenser novel Robert B. Parker has ever written, the opportunity occurs when a new client walks into Spencer's office, leading to the new situation — he begins his investigation.

Very often geography will follow structure in this regard — notice how many movies and novels change the location of the story right after the opportunity, so the hero begins a literal, as well as psychological, journey. Ann sets sail for Skull Island in *King Kong*; the animals leave the zoo in *Madagascar*; Bree leaves to find her son in *TransAmerica*. These new situations begin at the 10% point of each film.

Even if the story location remains the same, your hero must be placed in some new situation as the forward movement of the story begins. In many love stories and romantic comedies, like *Eternal Sunshine of the Spotless Mind*, *Fever Pitch* and *Shopgirl*, the heroes' involvement with their love interests is what gets the ball rolling. In all of these films, the two lovers begin dating at the 10% mark.

Entering this new situation creates a need for your hero to figure out what's going on, and to acclimate herself to her new surroundings or relationship. It is out of this New Situation that your hero's most important quality will emerge....

5. *What is your hero's OUTER MOTIVATION?*
If you've ever heard me lecture, or if you've read *Writing Screenplays That Sell*, you know that I consider the hero's goal the foundation of any story.

Stories are driven by *desire*. Whether it's finding the Golden Fleece, hunting the White Whale or solving the Da

Vinci Code, the hero's desire determines the plot and structure of the story.

In more than 90% of all Hollywood movies and TV episodes (and in the majority of books and plays), this desire is *visible*. It is easily envisioned as soon as we hear it, and it immediately establishes a finish line we're rooting for the hero to cross by the end of the film. Hence my term *Outer Motivation* — it is outwardly visible to the audience, as opposed to desires for self worth, acceptance, fulfillment or revenge, which are invisible.

It gets even more specific than that. Almost all Hollywood movies are about heroes pursuing one of only four visible goals:

- To win — either a competition, as in *Remember the Titans* and *Miracle*, or the love of another character, as in any love story or romantic comedy.

- To stop — meaning to stop something bad from happening, as in *Silence of the Lambs* or *Red Eye*.

- To escape — as in *Panic Room* or *The Island*.

- To retrieve — meaning to venture out and search for something of value, in order to bring it back safely, as in *Ransom* or *National Treasure*.

In addition to its richness of character, its statements about the nature of love and family, its examination of a controversial social issue and its universal themes, *Million Dollar Baby* is first of all a story about a fading fight manager who wants to guide a boxer to winning the world championship. Without that visible desire driving the plot, none of those other qualities, and none of the depth of the story, could emerge.

Perhaps because character and theme are fun to talk about after seeing a good movie or reading a good book, or because, as storytellers, we want our work to *mean* something, this basic principle is very difficult for many writers to master. They can talk endlessly about their stories' bigger themes, or what will make them visually stylish or politically charged, but they can't answer the simple question, "*What are we rooting for?*"

6. *What's the CONFLICT?*

Desire may drive your story forward, but the obstacles your hero faces are what elicit the greatest emotion. To get your reader to feel something as he reads your story, you must make it seem impossible for your hero to get what she wants.

This conflict can come from nature (*A Perfect Storm, The Grudge, Awakenings*), from other characters (*The March, The Plot Against America, Crash*), or from within the hero (*Walk the Line, A Beautiful Mind*, and any other story where the character goes through an emotional arc). But whether it's from the sheer power of the external obstacles, the chasm that divides the two lovers or the characters' own inner flaws and emotional fears, when buyers hear your pitch, you want them to immediately think, "*There's no way this hero can possibly win.*" Then they'll read your script to find out whether — and how — your hero succeeds in spite of all that conflict.

7. *What is your hero's ARC?*

Character arc simply means a character's inner growth and transformation through the course of the story. How does your hero (and perhaps other characters in your story as well) change inwardly as he pursues the visible goals and faces the visible obstacles you've given him?

Character arc is a journey from fear to courage — from living an emotionally safe but unfulfilled existence to risking everything to find one's destiny. It's your character's transformation from someone who's defined by others (parents, the past, society) to someone who stands up for himself.

In *Shrek*, the hero may act as if his life is perfect, but living a solitary, isolated existence in a swamp, protected by a sign that says KEEP OUT, is really just his way of avoiding the pain of rejection that he's been subjected to since childhood. He's defined by a society that regards him as ugly, scary and incapable of love — and he buys into it.

This is the BEFORE picture of Shrek we're presented with in the setup. But his transformation comes when he befriends Donkey, and then falls in love with Princess Fiona. His desire for her is so great that he's willing to risk the thing that has terrified him most — declaring his love and risking rejection. So his arc takes him from isolation to connection, from a protected existence to living his destiny.

Your hero's arc must always be *universal*. Like Shrek, we all fear rejection, and we all must exhibit courage if we want to experience connection and fulfillment. This is how the hero's arc defines the theme of that film.

A hero's arc requires great emotional courage and takes the entire book or movie for the hero to achieve transformation from a self-involved existence to one of loving generosity in both the novel and the movie *About a Boy*; Daniel's journey from a physically and emotionally isolated agoraphobic to a man willing to face his fears in order to find true love and family in the novel *The Pleasure of My Company*; and Dewey's learning to take responsibility and to give up his own ambition for the sake of the students in *School of Rock*.

Of course, in some stories, the hero doesn't find that necessary courage. Michael Corleone in *The Godfather* and Truman Capote in *Capote* are examples of such tragic heroes.

And in some stories, there simply is no character arc. Your primary goal is to elicit emotion, and if the action is exciting enough and the visible conflict great enough to accomplish that goal, it isn't necessary to delve deeply into the inner needs and conflicts of your characters. But in most novels and films, especially dramas, love stories and romantic comedies, character arc is essential.

8. What deeper ISSUES does the story explore?

Don't confuse character arc and theme with your story's *message*. Some novels and films make political statements, revealing some social issue or injustice that the writer wants to expose and address. *The Day After Tomorrow* addresses global warming. *Erin Brockovich* paints a picture of corporate greed and corruption. *Crash* examines the tragic consequences of racism. And *Hotel Rwanda* makes a powerful statement about the West's complacency and moral failure in the face of African genocide.

But these are social and political issues, not universal themes. The hero of *Hotel Rwanda* is portrayed as a man who goes along to get along, who plays it safe and avoids making waves for the sake of his family and his own personal comfort and status. But by the end of the film he will evolve into a courageous hero who risks everything to protect and save the people taking refuge in his hotel.

This arc is universal; you don't have to be a victim of war or genocide to exhibit this same courage and transformation in your own life. To fully realize our humanity, we must all find the courage to risk or sacrifice the things most important to us — even our own lives if necessary — for the sake of the greater good. That's the theme of the film.

9. What are the successful ANTECEDENTS for your story?

At some point, with every writer or producer I ever coach, I ask the question, "What two or three recent books or movies can you point to and say, '*Because that made money, mine will make money*.'" Far too frequently, writers have no idea what to answer. And until they can, it will be almost impossible for them to sell their stories.

Mentioning successful stories that are similar in genre, tone, plot and/or demographic give buyers a much clearer picture of your own story's commercial potential. These reference points put buyers in a positive mindset. Subconsciously they're thinking, "*Yeah, I want a hit like that.*"

I once heard a pitch for a movie I thought had a lot of possibilities. "That could really be hilarious," I said. The writer looked at me like I'd just giggled during an execution, and revealed that the story was supposed to be a serious drama. Not surprisingly, the company I worked for didn't option the script.

This may speak more to my twisted sensibilities than to the quality of the project. Nonetheless, a couple of antecedents would have prevented the misunderstanding, and enabled me to consider the writer's story on its own terms.

Antecedents also give buyers a clearer sense of your story's emotional elements. So does having a couple stars in mind who could play your hero, in case a buyer asks you for casting possibilities. If you convey the idea that your movie shares common elements with *The Ring*, *Dawn of the Dead* and *Saw*, then they immediately understand that your script is for a moderately budgeted movie that will scare the crap out of people — and make truckloads of money doing it.

Movie financiers and publishers want to do everything they can to insure a profit on their investment. They do that by replicating success. As soon as they begin listening to your pitch, they're thinking about what other movies or novels have made money by following the same path that you're suggesting.

You want to do that work for them, by making it clear that yours is the next in a line of similar movies or novels that have turned into cash machines.

Sometimes writers, groping for even a single successful precedent for their story, will answer, "There aren't really any antecedents for my project. I want it to be completely original."

Wrong answer.

Hollywood isn't looking for total originality. Neither is Random House. They're looking for movies and books they know how to market. Certainly you want your story to be unique and interesting; buyers aren't really just looking for clones of other best sellers and blockbusters. But if you can't point to at least a couple recent hits that verify your story's commercial potential, you're gonna have a tough sell.

10. What is your PASSION for this story?

What do *you* love about this story? What grabs you emotionally? What made you want to commit at least a year of your life — probably a lot more — to writing and selling this? What makes it a movie you'd want to see? What makes this a great movie, or a great novel (not just an interesting story)? Why is it a movie that *has* to be made, or a book that *must* be published?

Your passion is not so much something you'll announce during a pitch; it's an *attitude* you'll convey with everything you say to the buyer. Passion is contagious, and your excitement, focus and tone of voice must all convey your enthusiasm for your story.

So there you have it — the ten most important elements of a novel or screenplay. But just to beat you over the head with Rule #1: *Don't try to tell your story.* A pitch — even a 60-second one — is not a race to see how many of these you can convey in a minute. Using the methods I'll outline in the next chapter, you will select only the ones which convey the essence of your story to buyers, the ones that will get them emotionally involved enough that they'll start to share your passion for it. When you do that, they'll demand to read it.

DESIGNING YOUR PITCH

2

O nce you've reviewed your story and defined the ten key elements, you must decide which of those elements you'll reveal in just 60 seconds, and how you'll do so in the most captivating way possible.

Selecting Your Key Story Components

The specific story elements you choose depend entirely on the nature of your screenplay or novel. If you've written a big action script, the outer motivation and outer conflict are far more important than the character arc or the social issues you explore. But character arc is an essential component of any film or novel where the conflict comes from within the characters, and doesn't require a villain or a ticking clock.

Both *Armageddon* and *The Squid and the Whale* portray parent/child conflicts. But if you were pitching the action movie, would it really matter that we hear about the hero's antagonism toward his daughter's boyfriend, as long as you tell us that a meteor is about to destroy the entire planet? Conversely, if you omitted the complex themes and characters when pitching the latter film, what would that leave you to talk about?

Given that *Road to Perdition* is about a hired killer, it would seem crucial to reveal why readers or audiences will empathize with its hero, just as the social issues raised by *Remember the Titans* would be essential to any description of that screenplay.

Even though the list contains ten elements from which to choose, there are four that I consider almost essential to any good pitch: *hero, outer motivation, conflict,* and *passion.*

Whatever your story is about, whatever the genre, theme or emotional impact, the first thing a buyer — or reader — wants to know is: _What are we rooting for?_ Without some sense of who the protagonist is and what desire drives the story forward, it's hard to even see it as a story.

Look at any random list of movie blurbs or plot descriptions on the Internet Movie Database or the _New York Times_ best seller list. Notice how in almost every one, the hero, and the hero's desire, is stated or clearly implied. And keep in mind that these are themselves pitches — supplied by the distributors and publishers to get you to see the movies or buy the books.

Since your primary goal is to elicit emotion, describing the major conflict — inner or outer — is critical. Because emotion is created primarily by the conflicts the characters face. The greater the obstacles a hero must overcome, the greater our emotional involvement.

Most desires are pretty familiar: finding true love; stopping some evil force; winning a contest; getting rich. It's the _obstacles_ that are much more likely to be unique to your story: the people or circumstances separating the lovers; the power of the villain, opponent or force of nature; the particular treasure, contest, business deal, prize, or verdict the hero longs for.

And finally, passion is contagious. How can you expect a buyer to commit hours of his valuable time reading your work (or paying someone to read it), if you don't seem that excited about it yourself? If you're not _absolutely convinced_ that your story will turn a profit at the box office or the book store, why are you wasting the buyer's time? Producers and publishers and agents have to create or represent money-making novels and films to stay in business. So make their jobs easy for them. Pitch them a story you're so passionate about that their resistance and skepticism will evaporate.

Many times I've spoken to development executives or agents who said, "_This story didn't really sound commercial at_ *all, but the writer was so positive and passionate, I just had to see it for myself.*" (You'll hear versions of this comment repeated several times in Chapter 12.) If that passion translates to the page, those scripts and book proposals are the ones that lead to deals.

Opening Strong

Once you've selected the elements of your story which clearly and succinctly convey its power and commercial potential, the next step is to formulate a pitch that will reveal those elements to the buyer.

To begin this process, I want to share my favorite opening for a 60-second pitch. I have countless examples of clients and lecture participants getting their work read using this opening. It immediately draws the listener into your story, and immediately accesses your passion for your project.

Simply begin your pitch with this sentence: "*I think the best way to tell you about my story is to tell you how I came up with this idea.*" And then you do just that.

Opening this way accomplishes several things.

First, it draws buyers out of the real world and into the fictional world you've created. It's the pitching equivalent of "*Once upon a time…*," alerting buyers that you're about to begin talking about the story itself, and giving them a chance to focus and to stop thinking about all the other book proposals stacked on their desks that they haven't read, or how they'd rather be home playing with their kids.

Second, this opening is a great way to overcome your initial nervousness and awkwardness (more about that in Chapter 7). Once you're relating what really happened when you got this idea, you'll be remembering that experience, instead of worrying about how well you're performing.

Finally, this one sentence gets you right into your passion. Because whatever grabbed you then — a real event, something from your past, a dream, a song, a combination of other movies — is probably still the thing you love most about the story. And as soon as you're focused on the elements of the story that hooked you in, your enthusiasm will start to come through.

Let's say your script is a historical piece — usually a very difficult genre to sell. But you're a history buff (or a sports fan), and one day you read about a down-and-out, over-the-hill fighter during the Depression who fought the heavyweight champion of the world.

So you ask yourself, "*Why, of all the boxing stories, of all the underdog stories, and of all the rags-to-riches stories I've seen, read and heard about, did this one capture my interest?*"

Perhaps it was the fact that this was a true story. Perhaps it was because you love boxing, or Cinderella stories, or perhaps because this fighter became a hero for the common man, a guy who faced the same poverty and despair as most of the rest of the country, but whose integrity, determination and courage gave a whole nation inspiration and hope.

Whatever the answer, *that's* what you've got to convey as you open your pitch. That's where your passion lies, and that's what will hook your listener. And at some point in the past, that's how the movie *Cinderella Man* was born.

Notice something else about those last couple of paragraphs. Just saying how you came up with this particular story would convey *seven* of the ten key elements: hero, empathy, setup, opportunity, outer motivation, conflict, and passion. And it would have taken you less than 30 seconds.

You'd still have 30 more seconds to offer antecedents, reveal political issues the script reveals about the Depression that have direct application today, delve deeper into the arc for the hero, discuss the love story that's an integral part of the story, or give more detailed information about the obstacles the hero faces and how he overcomes them.

Accolades

If the project you're pitching has already proven itself in some way, you want the buyer to know that. If your screenplay or novel has placed in the top three in a writing competition, for example, or if you have elements (major director or major star) or financing attached to your script, these should be revealed at the top of the pitch.

So instead of beginning by revealing how you came up with the idea, you might start by saying, "*The screenplay I want to tell you about won second place last year out of 1200 entries in the American Screenwriters Association Screenplay Competition. But I think the best way to tell you about it is to tell you how I came up with the idea....*"

If you're going to claim that talent or money is attached to the production, make sure it's for real. If you can't use the word *committed*, as in "Jennifer Aniston has committed to play the lead," or "I have 2 million dollars of a total budget of 5 million committed to the project," then just stick with revealing the story.

Statements like, "Reese Witherspoon has said she's interested in starring" or "I have a close relationship with an investor in Florida who has said he'll put up half the money" are all regarded as bullshit. Not because the buyer thinks you're lying, but because empty promises and vague expressions of interest get said by friends, agents and financiers all the time, as a way of putting you off while they keep their options open, just in case you *do* go out and raise some serious money.

Similarly, avoid mentioning responses you've gotten from other people. Saying, "This got great coverage at CAA" or "The editor at HarperCollins said this was the best first novel she'd ever read" or "My mom loved it" simply weaken your pitch. If someone in power has firmly committed time or money to the project, great. Everything else is irrelevant.

Finally, don't tell the buyer why this movie or book is going to be an instant blockbuster or bestseller. Buyers *hate* hearing declarations like, "This is gonna be bigger than *The Wedding Crashers* because it will appeal to the teen crowd and it's twice as funny" or "Do you know that more than 1 billion men around the world shave every morning? That's why my novel about the inventor of the safety razor is going to be *huge!*"

The Power of "*What if...?*"

Even if your story is fictional, it still might have grown out of real events you've read or heard about. Or maybe you came up with your idea by seeing common elements to lots of recent films, and going the opposite way, or by taking an everyday experience of your own and inflating it to make it exciting or hilarious. Then the question becomes, how do you segue from the source of the idea to the quality that makes it unique?

This is when you invoke the magical incantation "*What if?*"

"*What if a rich young woman fell in love with a penniless stowaway on a luxury cruise ship — and it turned out to be the* Titanic?"

Or, "*It's often been rumored that* The Graduate *was based on a real family in Pasadena. Well, what if a young woman discovered her mother and grandmother were the real life Elaine and Mrs. Robinson?*" I don't know if that's how Ted Griffin got people to read his screenplay for *Rumor Has It*, but it easily could have been. (Actually, Ted Griffin can most likely get anyone to look at anything by saying, "I wrote *Ocean's 11*." But Ted Griffin's probably not reading this book. And somewhere along the line he had to pitch his projects just like you do.)

So let's see how you can move from the "*Let me tell you how I came up with this idea...*" opening, to the "*What if...?*" segue, to relating the key elements of your story. As

not good enough, or of telling his father how he feels, or of standing up for himself, and he'll be required to face those fears as he makes this journey.

• Finally, my *passion* should begin to emerge when I talk about my own relationship with my father. (For the record, I just made this story up once during a lecture, including the "true" part about the distant father who collected baseball cards. My dad wasn't, and didn't, though he did own a popcorn-and-candy store when I was little, and used to bring me baseball cards whenever he got a new shipment.)

The only key elements I omitted were *issues* (because I can't see how this story reveals or examines any larger political or social situation) and *antecedents*.

But wait! There's more!

Dropping In Antecedents

Once you've designed your "how I came up with this" revelation, and linked it to your story with a "what if?" segue, it's easy to go back and slip in a couple antecedents. I could easily have begun the above pitch by saying, "*Let me tell you how I came up with this idea. I've always been a huge fan of movies about that moment when a child passes into adolescence or adulthood — especially 'odyssey' stories like* Stand By Me *or adult/child relationship stories like* About a Boy. *Now when I was a kid, my father and I ...*" And then I'd continue the pitch in the same way as above.

It's not as if either that novella and novel, or their film adaptations, have anything to do with baseball cards or dying parents. But both mix humor with seriousness, both are about preteen boys who come of age, and most of all, both were very successful.

Sometimes the phrase "*I've always been a fan of stories like...*" is all you need to reveal how you came up with your idea. It may, in fact, be all you have to offer if your script isn't based on personal experience or on something you read or heard about. But if you've written a movie or novel in your favorite genre, and given it a new twist or original hook, it's a great way to lead your buyer to the "what if?" segue.

To find antecedents for your screenplay, go to lists of recent movies that can be grouped by genre. The Internet Movie Data Base, Done Deal Pro, *The Studio Report: Film Development,* and Netflix all offer those kinds of groupings. So do a number of publishing and fiction writing websites (see Chapter 4). Or go to the appropriate section of your local video store or bookstore. Just be sure your antecedents are recent, similar and successful.

Adding Details

This baseball card pitch times out at about 60 seconds, so I probably wouldn't add more details. But if you've conveyed the essential elements of your story and still have time, add details that reveal more about exactly what obstacles the hero will face, and how he overcomes them.

I could have added more about how our ten-year-old boy meets the con artist, how he locates the card, how he attempts to persuade the billionaire to sell it to him and how the con artist tries to steal it. The more you can draw the buyer into the story with specifics, and the more conflict you can build, the stronger the pitch will be. Just as long as you don't exceed your 60-second limit.

Notice that I also slipped the title into the end of the pitch. It isn't essential that you give the title at all — the buyer will see it when they get the screenplay, and they aren't likely to remember it until then. But if it's catchy or power-ful, or if it clearly conveys some element of the plot, it's fine to include it.

Pitching True Stories

When you're pitching a screenplay or novel based on a true story, don't say so at the beginning. Wait until the end of your pitch, when that final revelation will pack the greatest emotional wallop.

The general assumption in Hollywood — at least in the feature film arena — is that true stories are period pieces, or "inspirational" stories, or both, and should be relegated to the domain of the art house film or the TV movie. Of course, this bias ignores the commercial success of *Remember the Titans* or *Erin Brockovich* or *Coach Carter* or *A Beautiful Mind* or *Walk the Line* or *King Kong*, but the prejudice exists, nonetheless. (Okay, I know *King Kong* wasn't a true story. But don't you kind of wish it was?)

When the first information buyers get is that your story is true, they're already thinking, "This is going to be a tough sell." But imagine if you pitch the story in a way that gets them emotionally involved by using the process I've outlined. Then, just when the buyers are thinking your story is pretty amazing, you hit them with, *"... and everything I just said really happened."*

Suppose our baseball card story were true. If the pitch began, *"This is the true story of a ten-year-old boy who learns his father has cancer...,"* already it sounds depressing, and ordinary, and like something you'd have seen on TV in the seventies.

But imagine the pitch is exactly what we already have, except that right at the climax we add, *"And what if I told you this whole story is true, the boy did find the baseball card, and I have the rights to his story?"* You've added one more reason for buyers to want to read it. They were already hooked, and now they get to add "based on a true story" to the opening credits.

Waiting to reveal that your story is true is especially important if you're the hero of your own story. To reveal immediately that your novel or screenplay is based on something that happened to you personally can be a kiss of death in a pitch, because most autobiographical screenplays and manuscripts are dreadful. The writer is too close to what happened to be objective, too emotionally involved to see that the mass audience won't have any interest, and too afraid to dig deep into the characters' psyches for fear of getting sued, looking bad, or making loved ones look worse.

But again, if you've hooked your buyer already, and convinced her that this is an exciting or hilarious story with real commercial potential, you can strengthen the pitch even further by ending with, "*Everything I just described really happened, and I was the one it happened to.*" Now the buyer assumes that your familiarity with this fascinating story makes you the perfect person to write it.

Mistakes, Blunders, and Bad Advice

Lots of people are out there giving lots of advice about how to pitch your story. Most of it's good, some of it's bogus, but all of it is based on the experience of the lecturer or panelist or consultant or friend who's dishing it out. The process I offer in this book is by no means the only way to get someone to read your script. It's just the one I've had the greatest success with, and the one I've seen work again and again with students and clients.

So I want to warn you about some techniques that are often recommended but (in my experience) are seldom effective, as well as some understandable but deadly mistakes many writers come up with all by themselves.

These are the things to avoid as you design your pitch:

- **Don't lead with your title.** Mentioning the title at the end of the pitch is fine, since the listener now can understand its connection to the story. But when your first words are the title, buyers not only don't know what you're talking about, they aren't even fully listening yet. Remember that your pitch follows a hundred other phone calls or (if you're at a conference or pitch fest) dozens of other pitches. The buyer has to be drawn into your pitch with a few words that aren't important for her to remember. This is one of the reasons the "*Let me tell you how I came up with this…*" opening is so effective. Nothing important is said until you have the buyer's attention.

Titles take a moment to think about to make any sense. Even titles as powerful as *Jaws* or *The Terminator* would make buyers pause to try to create some mental image, or formulate some thoughts about them. And while they're doing that, you're barreling ahead with important information about your story, and they're missing it.

If your title *isn't* catchy, if it doesn't even create an immediate image, it's just going to confuse the listener. If you began a pitch, "*Brokeback Mountain* is about two cowboys who fall in love while herding some sheep and…," I guarantee the buyer wouldn't understand or remember the title.

• **Don't lead with a question.** Sometimes writers think it's cute or clever to engage buyers by asking personal questions related to their plots. "Did you ever wonder what became of the person you went to your high school prom with?" a writer asked me once in a pitch. This writer didn't really care about the answer; he just forged ahead with his pitch: "Well, my hero did, and that's why he set out to find her in *Getting Her Back*, a hilarious story about…" Meanwhile I'm not even listening, because I'm sitting there fantasizing about my prom date, thinking, "I wonder what *did* ever happen to Carol Schunk?"

This technique might have worked if the writer hadn't directed the question at me: "I don't know if this has ever happened to you, but one day I started wondering whatever became of the girl I took to my high school prom. And I asked myself, '*What if...?*'" A pitch that began this way would have me involved immediately.

- **Don't lead with a log line.** A log line is a single sentence that conveys the basic plot of your story in the most succinct, powerful way. The beauty of a log line is that it encapsulates the story very quickly and tells the buyer, "This is how my story can be described in an ad, or on a bestseller list, or in *TV Guide.*"

   It's easy to see why this would seem like a great way to grab a buyer right out of the gate. The problem is that you haven't yet drawn him into your story; you haven't given him time to leave his world and enter yours before hitting him with your pitch. Once you reveal the log line, there will be little surprise or anticipation during the rest of your pitch.

   My longtime friend and associate Devora Cutler-Rubenstein suggests *ending* the pitch with your log line — summarizing the story so the buyer is left with its essential concept and marketability.

   This is a terrific idea. I really wish I'd come up with it myself.

   Using this technique, our baseball card pitch could stay just as it is, but conclude with, "*So my screenplay, The Last Mickey Mantle, is about a ten-year-old boy who goes on a journey to find the world's rarest baseball card for his dying father.*"

- **Don't name all your characters.** Identify your characters by function — boy (or "our hero"), father, billionaire, con artist — instead of giving them all names that the buyer won't be able to keep straight or remember.

If you truly believe it makes your story stronger, go ahead and name your hero. But let the rest of the characters stay anonymous. Remember, you've only got 60 seconds.

- **Don't use jargon.** Mentioning act breaks, midpoints and heroes is fine, but don't start tossing around terms you picked up in screenwriting books and lectures — even mine.

  As you can tell, I'm a great believer in the power of principles like Opportunity and Outer Motivation and Major Setback, but don't include those phrases in your pitch. You might sound like you're just following some formula, or that you're trying to seem superior, and unless the buyer is familiar with my terminology (or whoever's you're using), he might misunderstand what you mean.

- **Don't give away the ending.** Your goal is to entice the buyer to read your screenplay, in the same way a movie trailer is designed to get an audience to come see the movie. And no movie trailer would give away the ending of the story. You're more likely to increase a buyer's interest if you leave him hanging, wondering how your hero will ever overcome all the obstacles she faces.

  Emotion grows out of conflict. So the most emotional ending to the Revelation portion of your pitch is probably the moment where the hero faces the major setback or crisis point of the story (the end of Act 2 in a screenplay), followed by the log line.

  If the buyer then *asks* you how it ends, tell him. It shows he's engaged, and you don't want to be coy just to get him to read the script — it probably won't work.

  Ending the pitch at the major setback isn't a hard and fast rule anyway. If you're pitching a true story about a person who did the impossible, you may need to reveal what impossible thing he did, which tells the buyer that the hero is going to win in the end, and the story will probably be uplifting. It would be hard to pitch *A Beautiful Mind* without revealing that John Nash won the Nobel Prize in spite of his schizophrenia.

With stories like *A Beautiful Mind*, the emotion comes from wondering *how* the hero could ever have accomplished whatever he did in spite of the overwhelming odds he faced. And you'd also include the love story in your pitch, leaving the buyer wondering if John Nash was able to hold onto Alicia's love and keep his family together.

With many biographies or true stories like *Cinderella Man*, you don't have to reveal the outcome. The fact that Jim Braddock had even a shot at the heavyweight championship makes him remarkable. The reader can find out if he won by reading the screenplay.

* **Don't hype your story.** Let your story speak for itself, and give the buyer credit for seeing its potential. Don't proclaim that it will make a lot of money, or that it's hilarious, terrifying or a sure-fire Pulitzer Prize winner. And don't say that Tom Cruise is sure to want to star in it. As soon as you declare these superlatives, the buyer will assume they're not true.

* **Don't try to tell your entire story.** Wait a minute! Haven't we heard this before?

Yes, you have, and you might hear it 602 more times before this book is over. It's that important.

PRACTICE
3

Beffore you ever dial an agent's number or show up at a pitch fest, you must rehearse your pitch until it's so familiar that it comes across as natural, passionate and spontaneous.

Actors preparing for a performance rehearse so much that they go beyond memorization. They know their parts well enough that they're able to be *in the moment* on stage or in front of the camera. They're not struggling to remember lines, they're listening to, and engaging, the other actors they're performing with.

This is how you'll approach your pitch. You must be so comfortable with it that no matter what happens — nerves, interruptions or forgotten lines — you'll be able to stay in the moment: enthusiastic about your story and fully engaged with the buyer.

Trial Runs

After you've designed your pitch, get whoever you can — friends, family, co-workers and writers group members — to rehearse it with you. Have them listen without interruption, and then give you whatever reactions and comments they have. Then pitch it again a couple more times, trying to incorporate their suggestions.

Here are a few ways to make these rehearsal sessions as empowering as possible:

- **Record them**. This way you won't have to worry about remembering what your listeners said, or what exactly you did to prompt their comments. Hearing your pitch will also force you to come up with your own ideas about how to improve it, or how better to convey the essence of your story.

If you use a digital recorder, you can upload the sessions and listen to them on your computer as you rewrite your pitch. You can also practice memorizing it by downloading the recordings onto your iPod, or burning them onto a CD, to listen to in your car.

- **Time it.** You must hone your 60-second pitch down to … well, 60 seconds. Give your listener a stopwatch, and if it's running long, ask for suggestions about what to trim.

- **Use notes.** Even though you've memorized your pitch, don't depend on your memory. Notes are perfectly acceptable, both at rehearsal and during the pitch itself. That way if, in the heat of pitching, you stumble or get interrupted, just a glance down at your notes will get you back on track.

  A couple suggestions about notes. Use note cards, so you're not unfolding some big piece of paper as you begin your pitch. Number them, so if you drop them and they get out of sequence, your pitch won't sound like a Fellini film. And write big. You don't want to be searching through a bunch of fine print to find the place you left off.

  This brings us to the most important rule of notes:

- **DON'T READ YOUR PITCH!** Notes are fine. Reading a transcribed pitch is not. You won't be able to look the buyer in the eye, it'll seem like you don't know your own story, and any sense of excitement or enthusiasm will disappear. You've got to commit your pitch to memory, then rehearse it enough that you can make it sound natural.

  This rule holds true even if you're on the phone —

especially if you're on the phone. A buyer can tell within ten seconds if you're reading to her, and *that's* what she's picturing on the other end of the line, instead of the images your story should be creating.

- **Pitch to two people at once.** This will occasionally happen at pitch fests, so you want to be prepared. You'll also get your two listeners brainstorming together about how to improve it. And you'll be so nervous performing for two people that your actual pitch to a producer will seem easy by comparison.

- **Role play.** Have your rehearsal listener pretend to be a specific person you'll be pitching to. You'll address him as that person, acknowledge him for some specific thing he's done, and use any other appropriate methods from Chapter 8 to create a relationship with your (mock) buyer.

- **Answer questions.** When you've completed your pitch, have your trial run listeners ask whatever questions about the story they can come up with. This will prepare you for most of the questions buyers might ask, and will give you lots of experience thinking on your feet. You must be able to talk about your story naturally and confidently, not just deliver a memorized speech.

  Have your listeners time your answers as well, and practice limiting them to 10 seconds each. It does no good to have a succinct, 60-second pitch, and then take 3 minutes to answer a simple question. Lots more about this in Chapter 9.

A Shameless Plug

One of the best ways to rehearse your pitch is to hire a consultant to help you mold it into one you know will knock a buyer's socks off. A coaching session like this should only take 20 or 30 minutes, and will insure that you've mastered all of these elements. I know the coaching process works, because I've done it a hundred times, and my pitch coaching clients *always* get their material read.

A pretty obvious sales pitch, I know. But what can I say? It's something I do very well, I know it works, and this is the place in the pitching process you should consider it. My website, *ScreenplayMastery.com*, provides all the details.

TARGETING YOUR BUYERS

4

J ust as there is no book or movie, no matter how successful, that everybody likes, neither is there a single, universal market for every screenplay or novel. A positive response to your story requires finding the specific agents, producers, publishers and executives whose taste, experience and position match your project. It's your job to determine which buyers are most likely to want to read and acquire your story, and go after them.

The most accurate indicator of whether individuals or companies are appropriate targets is to look at their records. What have they produced (or represented or published)? What projects do they have in development? What have they said they're looking for? Getting this information is not really difficult if you're willing to do some detective work.

The research you do to find potential buyers will also be invaluable for establishing rapport during your pitch. As you will see in Chapter 8, the information you gather, or the referral you get, can also provide you with the common experience or acknowledgment that will open your pitch session.

Don't wait until your screenplay or manuscript is ready to shop before beginning this research. Start tracking down buyers as soon as you've come up with a story concept, and continue compiling target companies the entire time you're writing the story.

In fact, beginning your research immediately is an excellent way to determine if there *is* a market for your story. If you can't find any antecedents, or any publishers or producers who've recently bought similar projects, chances are your story is commercially challenged.

What follows is a list of the primary sources of information for targeting buyers, and for designing your marketing plan.

Contacts and Referrals

Having your screenplay or book proposal recommended by someone the buyer knows and respects is by far your best shot at getting it read. People you know in the film or publishing industries, members of your writers group, or even friends and relatives outside the writing world can provide you with information about who is looking for what.

Once you've determined the antecedents to your story, use them to get suggestions for possible buyers: "*Who do you think I should go after if I have a humorous romance novel in the style of Jennifer Crusie?*"

If your contact knows the buyer he's suggested personally, ask if he'd be willing to introduce you — to make a call on your behalf recommending you to the person in power.

If your contact says no, or if it's an inappropriate question because you already know it would put your buyer in an awkward position, or because your contact isn't familiar enough with your work to recommend it, then ask if it's okay to use his name when contacting the buyer directly. Telling a buyer that the President of St. Martin's Press suggested you contact her isn't the same as a recommendation from the President of St. Martin's Press. But it's still much stronger than a cold call.

Interviews

Producers, development executives, publishers and agents frequently participate in panel discussions at film festivals, writers conferences and book fairs. They also promote their books and films by appearing at Q & A sessions or special screenings sponsored by organizations like the Writers Guild, PEN or the Motion Picture Academy. These are terrific opportunities to hear what they look for in screenplays, the kinds of projects that interest them, and even how to approach them.

These public appearances have the added benefit of giving you specific comments and quotes you can use to personalize your approach to the executive. When you write a query letter (Chapter 6), it's important to reveal why you've chosen this particular buyer to tell about your story. Quoting an insightful or inspiring comment she made during an interview is an outstanding way to accomplish that goal. Acknowledging a buyer for something she said is also a great way to establish a relationship at the beginning of your pitch (see Chapter 8).

You don't even need to attend the event to benefit from what the buyer says. Conferences often make recordings of presentations available during or after an event, and speeches and panel discussions are usually written up in newspapers, newsletters or websites. Simply acquire the recording, or read the article, to get the information you need.

Articles and Reviews

Newspaper, magazine and internet reviews of books and movies always include the producers or publishers involved. So if you read a review of a gothic horror novel, and that's what you've written, add the publisher and the author's agent to your list of people to contact. (The agent's name won't be included in the review, but as I'll explain below, it's pretty easy to acquire if you know who the publisher is.)

One of my favorite websites is *newyorktimes.com*, because they've catalogued every recent review — and lots of old ones — that the paper has published, categorized by year. This list is a great reminder of movies or novels like yours that you may have forgotten about. Of course, you'll have to wade through a lot of obscure Norwegian art house titles to find the antecedents for your teen slasher movie. But when you do, you'll have important details about companies that might be interested in it.

The Hollywood trade papers — *Variety* and *The Hollywood Reporter* — provide articles about production companies and agencies; the people in power; option and purchase deals; which movies are in preproduction or production; and which films are doing well at the box office or at festivals. Both are available in print or online, though a subscription is expensive (see *The Internet* below).

Publishers Weekly, also available in print or online, offers the same kind of information for the book world: agents, publishers, recent deals, best seller lists and articles about the industry.

Periodicals like *ScriptWriter Magazine*, *Writer's Digest*, *Creative Screenwriting*, *Poets & Writers*, *Scr(i)pt*, *Writer*, *The Hollywood Scriptwriter,* and *Premiere* also offer reviews, articles and interviews that can lead you to additional markets for your story.

 ## Screenwriting Directories

The Hollywood Creative Directory publishes two directories I consider almost essential for marketing a screenplay or film project, plus a third that can be very helpful:

- *The Studio Report: Film Development* is the most valuable reference book this publisher offers to screenwriters (and the one I'd recommend most highly if your budget is limited). This guide lists all of the projects which have gone into development (have been optioned, purchased or commissioned), or which have achieved significant forward movement (such as going into preproduction) at any of the studios during the five months prior to that issue's publication.

  Of even greater value, the projects are cross-referenced by studio, production company *and genre*. So if you're writing a horror film, you have an immediate list of production companies you can target, because they already have other horror films in development.

You can also read the log lines of all these horror films, to make certain your plot hasn't already been created and sold by someone else, and to see how similar stories to yours have been described in a succinct, powerful way.

The directory also provides the names of the screenwriters for each project, enabling you to track down agents who have successfully sold horror films, and might be open to considering yours.

- *The Hollywood Creative Directory* lists over 2,000 film and television production companies, including staff members by title, contact information and credits. The book includes studio information, and lists of companies that have development and production deals with each studio.

If you've come up with a movie that's an antecedent for your story, and you know the company that produced it, this directory will tell you the name and title of the head of development for the company, his business address and phone number, other movies the company has produced, and whether they have a deal with a studio.

The Hollywood Creative Directory is also cross referenced, so if you hear an executive speak at a conference, or if he's listed as one of the buyers at a pitch fest, you can look up all his contact information.

- *The Hollywood Representation Directory,* also published by the Hollywood Creative Directory, offers the same kind of information about agents, managers and entertainment attorneys in LA and New York. It's very helpful, but not as valuable as the two previous directories, since information on agents and managers is available — with more detail — at several online sites (see *The Internet* below).

- *The Spec Screenplay Sales Directory* contains more valuable information on all of the spec sales that occurred over a period of ten years, beginning in 1994: title, author, log line, agent, manager, producer, attorney, sales price and studio. These elements are cross-referenced, so if you're writing a romantic comedy, you can look up every romantic comedy spec sale, see who the agents and producers were, look them up, see what else they bought or sold, and target the ones that best suit your project. Then you can look them up in one of the directories above, or through many of the websites below, and make your contact.

  Unfortunately, as I'm writing this, *The Spec Screenplay Sales Directory* is no longer being published with up-to-date information. But the information that was compiled through 2004 is currently available at *hollywoodlitsales.com*. And perhaps as you read this, they've resumed publishing.

Publishing Directories

For book authors, *The Writer's Market* is probably the best known and most comprehensive directory for acquiring information on publishers and agents, the types of books of interest to each publisher, and suggestions on the whole process of marketing your book.

This directory also contains a lot of stuff about magazine writing that doesn't pertain directly to novels, but which you might find valuable for putting food on the table while you finish your epic about ancient Greek vase painters. Magazine articles have to be pitched like everything else, and soon you're going to be very good at it.

Here is a (far from complete) list of other books and directories for novelists and book authors, all of which include contact information on agencies and publishers, plus their own suggestions on marketing your work. There are many more guides and directories for particular markets and genres: romance writers, Christian writers, children's writers, mystery writers, children's mystery writers. This list could be endless, so I've concentrated on just a few of the general directories.

Many of the titles below include the year of the latest edition available as I write this. But again, there might be more recent editions available when you track them down.

- *The 2006 Guide to Literary Agents* by Kathryn S. Brogan (Editor), Robert Lee Brewer (Editor), and Joanna Masterson (Editor)

- *The Agents Directory* by Rachel Vater

- *Agents, Editors and You: The Insider's Guide to Getting Your Book Published* by Michelle Howry (Editor)

- *Jeff Herman's Guide to Book Publishers, Editors & Literary Agents, 2006: Who They Are! What They Want! How to Win Them Over!* by Jeff Herman

- *The Novel & Short Story Writer's Market 2006* by Lauren Mosko

Video Dealers

In looking for possible buyers for your screenplay, go down the rows of boxes at your favorite video rental store. Most of them categorize their films by genre, so first target the movies that might be antecedents. You don't have to rent anything; just jot down the key people involved in producing the film, then go home and research the production company in detail using all these other tools.

Write down the writers, stars and directors of the appropriate films as well. Many stars and directors have their own production companies, which you can approach like any other with your pitch. And it's easy to find out who represents any particular producer, director or screenwriter (see *The Internet* and *Telephone Research* below), and then pursue that agent or manager, either because you have a project that's perfect for her client, or because you're looking for representation.

Finding lists of movie titles, and the filmmakers involved, is even easier (and offers you a bigger selection) if you simply go to *netflix.com* or *blockbuster.com*. These sites also allow you to look up titles by genre.

I know this isn't directly related to pitching, but I also *highly* recommend subscribing to Netflix if you're pursuing a screenwriting career. You should certainly be viewing a minimum of two movies a week, particularly those within the genre of your own screenplay. This is the most convenient way to do it, and the one with the most available choices.

Book Dealers

If you're researching book buyers or literary agents in the publishing world, go back to the preceding section, and substitute "Book Stores" for "Video Dealers." And replace Netflix and Blockbuster with *Amazon.com* (or whichever of the many bookselling sites you prefer). You can then track down an author's agent as easily as you can a screenwriter's (again, see *The Internet* and *Telephone Research* below).

Pitch Fest Lists

Pitch marts, writers conferences and film festivals offer great opportunities to pitch your project to a lot of buyers, face-to-face, in a very short time.

These events can also be a great source of leads to other potential buyers. But I can get in big trouble for recommending what I'm about to, so *please don't tell anyone you heard it from me*....

If there's a company on a pitch fest list that you're not able to meet because their time slots are all booked, or because you didn't learn about them soon enough, just wait until a week or so after the conference, then write, email or telephone them directly. You know they're in the market for novels or screenplays because they sent a rep to the pitch fest. And it's unlikely they'll have heard so many good stories that they're no longer looking for material.

You won't get to pitch your story to a buyer in person, but chances are good that someone at the company will be willing to talk to you, especially if you say how much you wanted to meet with them, and that your pitch will only take a couple minutes.

Now here's the sneaky part: *you can do this even if you didn't attend the pitch fest.* Simply get a list of the companies that were scheduled to be there, either from the conference promotional materials or from a friend who attended. At the very least, get the list of who attended the previous year's conference; these companies are always listed in the advertising for the current pitch fest. Then contact them directly as I just described.

Please don't misunderstand — I'm not trying to dissuade you from attending writers conferences or book fairs or film festivals or pitch fests. They provide opportunities you wouldn't otherwise have, to meet people in power and to pitch your material. And phone calls just aren't as effective as face-to-face meetings.

But no writer or filmmaker has the time, money and geographic proximity to attend every event on the calendar. So here's a way to expand your marketing list beyond the conferences you do attend.

I certainly don't want to diminish the success of pitch fests and writers conferences; their sponsors work tremendously hard to offer writers invaluable industry access they wouldn't otherwise have. Plus I have close relationships with the organizers of many of these events. Or at least I did have, unless one of you squealed, and now they won't talk to me. But my primary commitment with this book is to suggest every way possible to get your story read. And this is another way.

The Internet

The web is now the best single source of information writers have for finding and researching potential buyers. It's current, it's huge, and it's really cheap. So it's absolutely essential that you surf through as many sites as possible in your quest for potential buyers.

There are dozens of great websites for getting the kind of information you need to market your story. Unfortunately, if you're reading this book years after it was written (and I fully expect it to be in print for decades), some of these sites may no longer exist. Certainly, others will have come along which might be even more valuable. So in addition to the sites I offer, keep surfing and networking to find additional resources for targeting buyers.

The list below emphasizes sites that offer specific credit and contact information on buyers. But many of these sites (including a few of my favorites that aren't "directories") contain articles, contest info, resources, member discounts and lots of other goodies that can help advance your writing career.

My apologies to any site I've neglected to mention because I'm not yet aware of it, or because there are simply too many to include them all. It's no reflection on the value of your site. This is just a partial list of what I know is out there right now (minus the http, the //, the www, the .html, and all those other extra letters and slashes).

• Done Deal Pro (*donedealpro.com*). This invaluable site tracks script, book, treatment, and pitch sales and options on a daily basis. More important, subscribers can search a sales database of over 7000 deals by title, writer, writer's agent or manager, company, and genre. For each individual sale listed, users can click on agency, management firm, law firm and company names to find contact information, companies' interests (i.e. preferred genres), submission policies and type of material accepted, as well as staff member names.

In other words, if you've written a screenplay about a heist, you can do a genre search on "caper" (it's that specific) and get information on all the caper movie screenplays (including development deals, not just produced films) sold or optioned since 1997. (Out of curiosity I just did that search, and found 13 caper script listings, including the names and contact information for the production companies and agents involved.)

Done Deal Pro has added goodies, like a free newsletter, development-related industry news, interviews, a searchable database of screenwriting contests and contest deadline alerts. If your budget limits you to only one paid subscription site (as of this writing, it's only $23.95 a year), I'd make it this one.

• The Internet Movie Database (*imdb.com*). This is a simply amazing site, offering listings of pretty much every American movie ever made, plus lots of foreign ones and TV shows as well, along with log lines, tag lines, release dates, artists involved, cast lists (including character names), and reviews.

• *IMDbPro.com.* For a small monthly fee, you get access to this premium section of the IMDb site. It will provide you with everything mentioned above, plus any available representation and contact information for the writers, producers, directors and stars listed. If you plug in the code *screenplay05*, you can get a one-month free trial to check it out.

- *boxofficemojo.com.* An essential source for estimating just how profitable your antecedents were, so you're not referencing any box office disasters in your pitch.

- *hollywoodlitsales.com.* Also mentioned in the *Directories* section above. Check it out to see if the information from *The Spec Screenplay Sales Directory* is available, plus other info about potential buyers and upcoming pitch fests.

- *hollywoodreporter.com* and *variety.com.* The two main film industry trade papers are also available, by subscription, on line. Better than print subscriptions, because it saves trees, and it's easier to research past issues online (unless you want to be seen reading *The Hollywood Reporter* in your local Starbucks, so people will be impressed that you're in the biz).

These sites are your best sources for the latest information on the film and television industries — executive shuffles at the studios, foreign and domestic box office and ratings, reviews, gossip, stock prices, and a whole lot of other stuff you won't need in order to market your script, but which you might find interesting. These are very expensive resources compared to the other subscription sites, although each offers a free one-month trial subscription.

Just those seven sites will provide you with more information than you can probably handle on prospective targets for your screenplay. But I've added some additional sites below that are great sources of information on the craft and business of screenwriting:

- *ScreenplayMastery.com*. This is my website. That's why it's listed first.

- *goasa.com*. This free website, and *Script Notes*, the American Screenwriters Association monthly newsletter, are filled with lots of good information. But my real reason for listing this site is to urge you to join the organization (I'm on their Board of Directors).

  Membership offers lots of perks, including discounts on products and services, a discounted entry fee for their annual screenwriting competition, a script registration service, and reduced admission to Selling to Hollywood, one of the best screenwriting conferences in existence.

- *wordplayer.com*. This site is written by Terry Rossio and Ted Elliott, who wrote *Shrek*, *The Mask of Zorro*, *Aladdin*, all three *Pirates of the Caribbean* movies, and a bunch of other huge hits. The wonderful articles offer an insider's look at the craft of screenwriting, as well as examining the entire process of building and maintaining a career in Hollywood.

- *creativescreenwriting.com*. In addition to the monthly magazine mentioned above, *Creative Screenwriting* — sponsor of the annual Screenwriting EXPO and its PitchXchange — offers information and past articles on their website. You can also subscribe to their free e-zine, *CSWeekly*, which offers more information and advice, plus interviews with successful screenwriters who reveal how they practice their craft, and how they successfully broke into the business.

- *writersstore.com*. This is the best single source of books and software on all aspects of writing. They also have a great monthly e-zine that's free. But mostly I want to mention them because they're terrific people, and have always been really supportive. So they deserve it.

- *ScreenplayMastery.com*. This is still my website. That's why it's listed twice.

Fiction Writing Websites

These sites all offer listings and contact information on agents and publishers, as well as articles, advice and information on the publishing industry. Again, this list is by no means exhaustive. There are countless other fiction sites which offer great information, but which don't provide listings of potential buyers, so I didn't include them. This is just a starting point for additional web research you'll do as you gather information appropriate for your work.

Just a reminder, many of the agencies and publishers listed in these sites, and in the directories above, say they won't consider new clients or accept unsolicited material. But if they seem ideal for your book proposal, you're going to pursue them anyway, right?

- *Publishers Weekly* (*publishersweekly.com*) is the place I'd start any research into the publishing world. It's huge, with lots of information on all aspects of the industry, though not as targeted, and without some of the services, as the sites that follow.

- The Association of Authors' Representatives (*aar-online.org*). This is a nonprofit organization for independent literary and dramatic agents. It has a database and FAQs, plus articles and links. The listings include agent names, agencies, addresses, and sometimes email addresses, submission guidelines, genres represented and whether or not they're accepting new clients.

- *authorlink.com*. An abundance of information and links on all aspects of writing and marketing your book proposal. Some of it's free, but to access agent directory listings and other offerings requires a small monthly membership fee ($6/month as of this writing). The site also includes more expensive membership levels, including opportunities for critiques, and to showcase your work (see *Internet Listings* in Chapter 6).

- *bookpitch.com.* An extremely comprehensive site offering information and guidance and all aspects of getting your work published. Also offers showcase opportunities for your work (see *Internet Listings* in Chapter 6).

- Book Wire (*bookwire.com*). With all kinds of information on the entire publishing industry, this can be a good resource for finding out who's publishing what, and tracking down publishers by genre.

- *FictionAddiction.net.* I find this site to be really simple and straightforward, unlike some of the others that offer so much information it's hard to slog through it all. This one has agent and publisher info, publishing news and articles on all aspects of fiction writing and selling.

- *forwriters.com.* This site offers links to markets, including publishing houses, magazines and periodicals, and internet sites that buy fiction, as well as some agencies. There are also links and/or information on reference sites, writers groups, conventions, author sites and forums.

- Spec Fiction World (*specficworld.com*). is geared mainly to Science Fiction, Horror and Fantasy writing, though it provides some contact information on agencies and publishers outside those genres. It also offers advice on writing, links to other fiction writing sites, and information on books about writing, forums, rights and contracts, upcoming conventions, writing workshops, book distributors and search engines for writers.

Telephone Research

Here are a couple other methods for tracking down agents or buyers, if your other research hasn't gotten you to them.

Let's say you've looked at film credits for three period love stories, and now have the names of five separate screenwriters. You know that whoever represents them is probably open to marketing scripts in that genre, since they've already done it successfully.

To find the names and contact information for their agents, call the Agency Department of the Writers Guild of America. They'll give you the names of the writers' agents (or lawyers or managers, if the writers have no agents). Then look up those agents' contact information on *donedealpro.com*, *IMDbPro.com* or in the Hollywood Creative Directory *Representation Directory* (see above). And of course, see if they're crossed referenced in the *The Studio Report: Film Development* or at *donedealpro.com*, to learn what projects they've recently represented and sold.

To find a book author's agent in the same way, phone the publisher of his book, ask for the subsidiary rights department, and ask who represents the author or who represents the film rights to the book. This will usually lead you to the agent or attorney who negotiated his deal.

Sometimes you can find out which agency represents a writer, but not the name of the individual agent. In that case, just phone the agency switchboard and ask.

Similarly, if you don't know the most appropriate person at a production company to target, and the directories above don't make it clear, just phone the company and ask, "*Who is in charge of development for your company?*" If the person who answers doesn't know, just say, "*Who would be the best person at the company for me to contact about a screenplay I have the rights to?*" This is true by the way — you do own the rights to your own screenplay — and is usually a more effective way of getting the answer you want from the receptionist than telling him you're a screenwriter.

If you can't find a particular production company, call the switchboard for the studio that distributed the producer's most recent film, and ask if they have a number for the company. Often the producer has an office on the lot, or has left a contact number.

And of course, there's always directory assistance. Almost every Hollywood production company and agency will be found in the 213, 323, 310, 424, or 818 area codes.

If you can't locate a specific agent or company through your contacts, the directories and websites listed above, or by calling the publishers, the guilds, the studios and directory assistance, the buyer has probably moved on to selling Amway, real estate or drugs, and isn't the best target for your pitch anyway.

PUTTING THE TOOLS TO WORK

5

S
o now that you've done more research than you did in
four whole years of college, what do you do with all
this information? How do you turn lists of names,
titles, companies, credits and box office receipts into a plan
of action?

Targeting the Right Executive
When you've selected a producer or publisher you want to
pursue with your screenplay or book proposal, be sure to
identify the right individual to approach at that company.
Unless you have a personal relationship with someone
higher up the food chain, the development executive at the
production company is the person to contact. This could be
the Director of Development, Vice President of Creative
Affairs, Story Editor or any other title that implies that this
person's job is to find publishable manuscripts, or screenplays
with production potential.

At publishing houses, look first for editors — preferably
those who were involved with the novels you're using as
antecedents.

Agencies don't work quite the same way; if you identify
an agent who you've heard speak at a conference, or who has
successfully represented a writer with a project similar to
yours in genre or demographic, pursue that agent directly.

Large agencies also have story editors — people who
manage the staff of readers, but who aren't agents themselves.
These individuals are excellent prospects to target, because if
they read your material and like it, they can direct it to the
most appropriate agents at their companies.

And don't neglect the possibility of contacting assistants

and readers at any of these companies directly. These are usually the people who will end up reading your work initially anyway. If they can be persuaded to look at your project, and they like it, their bosses will hear about it. Remember, your goal is ultimately to get *anyone* at any of your target companies to read your stuff.

Of course, if you attend a pitch fest, you get whoever the buyers send. This isn't necessarily a bad thing. Even if they haven't yet reached powerful positions with their companies, their job is to hear pitches and screen material. And they're *desperate* to find good scripts, because it's the best way for them to advance their own careers.

Pitch Fest Research
A frequent problem at conferences and pitch marts is having no opportunity to research a buyer. The final list of companies in attendance is handed to you the morning of your pitch. Companies don't show, new ones get added at the last minute, or openings for pitching slots open up, and all of a sudden you're signed up to pitch a buyer you've never heard of, or who you didn't know would be there.

To prepare for this, have as many resources available as you can: bring a notebook computer, pda or cell phone with remote internet access; have copies of at least one or two directories with you; have a friend or significant other with internet access standing by at home to look stuff up for you; ask other attendees if they know anything about the company; and of course, read the company blurb provided by the festival sponsors.

If you simply can't find any information about a company prior to meeting them, simply acknowledge the person for being there, and launch into your pitch. What's the worst that can happen? So what if you discover you're pitching your slasher movie to a Christian cable network? It'll still be good practice.

The 10 Steps to a Powerful Hit List

Armed with all of the resources outlined in the previous chapter, you're now well equipped to design a targeted list of the strongest possible buyers for your screenplay or novel. The process outlined focuses a lot on movies and books similar to yours in genre. But don't limit yourself to that criteria. If a company has produced or published several of your favorite films or books, add them to the list. And add anyone a contact recommends as well, or anyone you hear speak, or learn about in your research, who impresses you, or has a great reputation, or is actively looking for a variety of projects, or who just seems like they're worth a shot.

Many buyers don't want to be involved in the same kind of project over and over, and you might come along just when they've decided to do a story like yours for the first time. So when in doubt, track them down. It's better to have a list that's too long than too short.

Here are the ten basic steps to tracking down the specific people you're going to approach:

1. Once your story is far enough along that you feel comfortable telling people about it, prepare a short log line or 10-second pitch *as you continue writing it*. (Don't wait until it's ready to submit to begin tracking down potential buyers.)

2. Contact all the people in your network who *aren't* potential buyers (you'll save them for when your script or book is ready), and give them your log line. Then ask if they can suggest any appropriate antecedents you may not have thought of, and if they can recommend any agents, producers or publishers they know, or have heard of, who they think would be appropriate for you to contact when it's ready.

3. Go to sources like *newyorktimes.com* to look through their lists of movie or book reviews for the last few years to see what additional antecedents you can spot.

4. Do a search for titles in your genre on *amazon.com*, *netflix.com*, *imdb.com*, *publishersweekly.com*, *bookwire.com* and/or *forwriters.com* to complete your list of published or produced antecedents for your story.

5. Now go to back to *publishersweekly.com* (for your novel idea) or to donedealpro.com and *The Studio Report: Film Development* (for your movie idea) to read about what recent deals have been made for books and screenplays within your genre.

You should now have a lengthy list of antecedents and projects in development. Now you want to research each title one by one to find the names of the key buyers involved in each project: the authors' representatives, and the production companies or publishers.

6. For those sites that have direct links to contact information on the buyers involved, add those addresses, phone numbers and emails to your list.

7. For buyers whose contact information isn't listed, go to directories like the *Hollywood Creative Directory* or *The Writer's Market*.

8. For companies where the individual agent or editor isn't identified, phone the company switchboard and ask who it is.

9. If you can't identify the writer's representative in any other way, call the publisher of the novel or the Writers Guild of America and ask.

10. Finally, go back to all the appropriate resources and search for the buyer's other projects, to get a better sense of the individual's taste and track record, and to accumulate information for establishing rapport.

Follow these ten steps throughout the writing process, and I guarantee you'll have a long, targeted list of potential buyers to contact once your screenplay or book proposal is ready to submit.

SECURING OPPORTUNITIES TO PITCH

6

Once you've prepared and rehearsed your sensational pitch, and have selected your target buyers, just one hurdle remains: *How do you get them to listen to it?*

An Editorial Comment...

Since the beginning of humanity, people have used stories to elicit emotion, to express their deepest beliefs and feelings, to inform, to anger, to amuse, to inspire, and to advance civilization. And as soon as the first Neanderthal told the first story to the first cavemen huddled around a fire, another Neanderthal was saying, "*Gee, I'd love to do that, but I don't know anyone who produces fires.*"

The #1 excuse for failure among writers is that they can't sell their stuff without an agent, and they can't get an agent without having sold anything.

It's also the #1 crock of shit.

A popular variation of this Catch-22 excuse is to claim that it's impossible even to get a screenplay or manuscript read if you don't know somebody powerful in Hollywood or New York or Toronto or London or wherever.

My answer to these excuses is always to pose this question: "*If it's impossible to get stuff read, how do any stories ever get sold, or books printed, or movies made? Were all those writers just the children of publishers and movie stars?*"

Getting your story read, and getting your pitch heard, isn't *easy*. It takes thought, preparation, effort and tenacity. But it's far from impossible — just ask all the agents and readers who lug a dozen scripts or book proposals home every weekend. The authors of those stories somehow got it done.

If you don't know anybody when your story is ready to market, you go meet people. You introduce yourself to the people in power with a referral, or a letter, or an email, or a phone call, or at a pitch fest or at a conference or at a party. And if any of the people you want to meet simply aren't accessible, you go meet people who are close to them, and you get them to read your story, and you trust that your writing will speak for itself, and is powerful enough to get in the hands of the people you want to see it.

And how, exactly, do you do all that? How do you persuade these powerful people to hear your pitch? I'll tell you how....

But Wait, I Have One More Rant...
Sooner or later — probably sooner — as you begin implementing the steps outlined in this book, you're going to hear someone say, *"Agents won't listen to pitches. You've got to send a query letter."* Then you'll go to a writers conference, where you'll hear a panel of agents say, *"We won't listen to pitches over the phone. You've got to send us a query letter."* And then you'll read a book or an article or a web posting that says the same thing.

And pretty soon you're in danger of excusing yourself from even preparing a pitch, let alone going after potential buyers, because you've convinced yourself that a query letter is all that matters.

I don't deny that query letters are important. I'll talk about them shortly. And I know it's the stated policy of almost every agency, production company and publishing house in the country to require query letters, just as it's the stated policy of almost every producer and studio in Hollywood not to accept screenplays unless they're submitted by agents.

But here's my question: If you ask every single one of these agents or producers or editors if, in spite of company policy, they have ever agreed to look at a screenplay or book proposal without first seeing a query letter, will you find a single one whose answer will be no?

Not likely. Everyone in power, because of a recommendation, or because of a persuasive writer who caught them on the phone after her assistant had left, or because of an interesting or passionate writer she met at a conference or party, has broken that "rule" and listened to a short pitch. And because that pitch hooked her immediately, she agreed to read the writer's story.

You just have to become that writer.

You won't get lucky with everyone. But like every other aspect of marketing your writing, you're playing a numbers game, and the more people you approach, the more successful you'll be.

Referrals

The strongest way to approach potential buyers, and the most likely way to get your story read, is with referrals from people the buyers know and respect. They don't even have to respect them that much. If someone vouches for your ability as a writer, or for the strength of your story, the buyer *wants* to believe him.

Though it's easy to forget in the face of all the stories of rejection you hear, agents and managers and publishers and producers *want* to find good writers, and good stories. They have to, or they're out of business.

The reason it's often hard to get stuff read is that the people in power are incredibly busy, and they simply don't have time to wade through every unsolicited screenplay or manuscript they encounter — especially when such a tiny percentage is worth reading.

So when a writer is recommended to her, an agent is interested, because it means somebody else has done the work of slogging through all the junk written by all the time-wasters to find a storyteller with potential. It's at least worth her time to hear a 60-second pitch, so she can make up her own mind.

A referral doesn't require that the person making the recommendation read your script (although it's an even stronger recommendation if he does). You can call your contact and say, *"I've just finished my latest screenplay, and I'm wondering if you know anyone you think might be interested in this particular story."* When they ask what it's about, you simply launch your 60-second pitch.

Hearing the essential components of your story will make it much easier for your contact to identify potential buyers. And because your pitch has hooked him emotionally, he'll feel far more comfortable recommending you to people he knows.

A referral doesn't require that your contact actually make the introduction. Once he suggests possible buyers for you to pursue, ask if it's okay to use his name in making your pitch. This will often be enough to get a buyer to hear your story.

One word of caution: Never *ever* claim a recommendation if you haven't actually gotten permission from the person you claim referred you. It's dishonest, and it can end up embarrassing or angering everybody involved. That will damage your reputation and career far more than not getting a particular buyer to read your script.

Pitch Festivals

Without pitch fests, this book would never have been written. I've been lecturing about writing, and coaching writers on their work, for more than twenty-five years. So when pitch fests came along, lots of my students and clients wanted to know how to take advantage of this new opportunity.

Because most pitch fests allow only five minutes with a buyer, the old rules of pitch *meetings* didn't really apply. And

I knew what a struggle it was for most writers — even those with terrific stories — to describe their work succinctly, while conveying its commercial and artistic potential. So I began working with writers one-on-one to create pitches that would get buyers interested. The more writers I coached, the more I realized that the weaknesses of bad pitches — trying to tell the whole story, focusing on unimportant details, neglecting the need for passion and emotion — showed up again and again. So out of that grew a lecture about designing and presenting a great pitch. And out of that lecture grew this book.

So, understandably, I consider pitch fests (or pitch marts, or one-on-ones with agents and editors at conferences and book fairs) great opportunities for writers to get access to buyers that might otherwise be hard to reach. Nonetheless, there are three big drawbacks to pitch fests:

• **Pitch fests are expensive.** Pitch fests generally require a sizable flat fee for an unlimited number of pitches, or a "per pitch" fee that can add up quickly if you're pitching to lots of buyers. This means that you want to be absolutely certain that your pitch is powerful and well rehearsed before you arrive.

Equally important, it means that your screenplay or manuscript is absolutely professional quality *before you begin pitching*, so that if you get interest (and if you use the methods in this book, I guarantee you will), you've got a good shot at getting a deal.

Unless you've gotten consistent positive feedback from people whose judgment you trust (because they're knowledgeable about fiction and because they'll be honest about your story's weaknesses), attending a pitch fest is premature. Keep saving up your money while you continue rewriting.

Some screenwriters attend pitch fests and pitch projects they haven't even completed. If the purpose of doing this is to secure a development deal to get paid to write the script, it's a big mistake. Unless you're a well established writer — and if you are, pitch fests aren't necessary — you won't get a writing deal based only on a pitch or a treatment. You must have a completed screenplay.

Pitching a story without a completed screenplay really only makes sense if you want to co-produce the project, and you're looking for representation, or for a production company to partner with. Having no screenplay can sometimes be an advantage in this case, because it allows the company to bring in an established screenwriter and offer him sole writing credit. But it won't advance *your* writing career.

Of course, if you're a novelist, you'll be pitching unfinished work most of the time, because your goal will be to get a book proposal read, not a completed manuscript. Just make sure you've gotten lots of positive feedback on the proposal, and don't pitch your story until *that's* ready to submit.

I suppose it's logical to pitch your uncompleted project to get a feel for how buyers will react to your story before you commit many more months to writing it. If you can afford to do this, great. But it's an expensive way to test the marketplace.

• *Pitch fests require lots of travel.* No way around this, unless you live in Southern California (a high price to pay just to be close to pitch fests). So now issues of cost become even greater.

If you have to take time away from home, and pay all those travel costs, I'd focus on pitch fests that offer lots of pitching opportunities for one flat fee, like the Great

American Pitch Fest (for screenwriters) and the New York City Pitch-and-Shop Conference (for novelists), or which are held in conjunction with a writers conference, so the trip offers lots of educational and networking opportunities, e.g. the American Screenwriters Association Selling to Hollywood Conference and the Screenwriting EXPO-PitchXchange (for screenwriters); the Romance Writers of America national conference and Book Expo America (for book authors); and the Willamette Writers Conference and Santa Barbara Writers Conference (for both). Many more pitching opportunities exist in all of these categories, and can be found with a little web surfing.

- *The top agents and executives from the most powerful companies don't usually show up at pitch fests.* No way around this either.

The majority of people you'll pitch to at any legitimate pitch fest have the ability to lead you to a deal. But some big agencies don't allow their people to participate in pitch fests. And some production companies and publishers assign the newest readers and assistants to hear pitches, often insisting that they only collect synopses of the pitches they hear, because they can't agree to read anything on their own.

But so what? If buyers won't come, they won't come. Pursue them using the other methods in this chapter.

And if you're pitching to a lowly assistant, give him your best pitch. As I've said, he's far more eager to find good material (and far more desperate to finally hear a good pitch) than an established agent, because the assistant knows bringing in good material is his best shot at getting promoted (and then sending *his* poor assistant to the next pitch fest).

Conferences and Book Fairs

Pitch fests are often one component of larger writers conferences and book fairs. But even if a conference has no official pitch fest, they provide a number of other opportunities to deliver your short pitch:

- *One-on-one sessions*. Participating in a conference often gives you the opportunity for 10- or 15-minute, face-to-face meetings with the speakers and panelists. But don't approach the session as if it's the same as a pitch fest encounter. Some of these people aren't in a position to acquire projects or read material. They're writers themselves, or have been instructed not to solicit or accept material for legal reasons.

  So when you begin your one-on-one, tell the person that you're marketing your story, and would like to get her feedback on your pitch. If she's in a position to read material, if your pitch is strong (which it will be), and if it sounds appropriate for her company, she'll ask to read it.

  If she can't accept material to read, you'll still get additional help honing your pitch. Then you can ask, *"Now that you've heard my pitch, who do you think I should contact about the project? What do you think is the best way to get to them?"* If the person is truly enthusiastic about your story, and suggests a specific person who might be interested, you can even ask if it's okay to use her name. *"When I contact [the person she recommended], may I say that you suggested I call?"*

  Always take a list of specific questions to these one-on-one sessions. If you have time remaining after your pitch, or if the person isn't willing to hear your pitch in the first place, the session will still be of great value.

  I know you didn't ask, but even if you're not pitching — *especially* if you're not pitching — always have questions prepared when you sit down with a guest lecturer or panelist.

I've done a lot of these table meetings at conferences, and the most frustrating situations are when writers arrive with no real sense of what they want to know. I don't mind asking, "How can our ten minutes be the most help to you?" but I always believe that if the writers had been prepared, I could have offered them much more valuable information and advice.

- *Hallway pitches*. Conferences offer many informal encounters with potential buyers. Though tackling an agent in the hotel lobby, pinning him against the wall and forcing him to hear your pitch might get you into trouble — or at least make it hard to establish rapport — there are less dramatic ways of introducing yourself and talking about your project.

The key is to respect the person's time. Tell him why you're eager to meet him, and then ask if there is any time that would be convenient to tell him about your story.

To begin your pitch on the spot is presumptuous, won't get the buyer's full attention and is likely to put him off. Instead say, "*I've been hoping ever since I heard your panel discussion that I'd get a chance to talk to you. I loved what you said about _____ (or I loved the novel you were involved in, or I was a big fan of the movie you helped get made). I have a novel (or screenplay) I'm just beginning to market, and I wondered if you had two minutes here at the conference, or over the phone, that I could tell you about it.*"

As you probably guessed, when you're in this situation, don't whip out a copy of your book proposal or screenplay as you walk up to the buyer. If you do, he'll assume you're going to ask him to take it on the spot, which he can't, or won't want to. So he'll probably pass on hearing your pitch altogether.

Otherwise, chances are good that unless he's surrounded by other people, or is late getting somewhere, he'll ask to hear your pitch right then. If he doesn't, he'll ask you to meet him later, or to phone his assistant the following week. But the choice is his, and either way, he'll respect your consideration and professionalism, which will make him that much more interested in the possibility of working with you.

- *Pitching workshops.* Some pitch fests or book fairs offer seminars where participants present their pitches just to get coaching from several experts. This is a great opportunity to rehearse your pitch. Not only will you get valuable suggestions on how to sharpen it, you'll be so nervous pitching to a room full of people that the pitches you make to buyers will seem easy by comparison.

   An added advantage to these classes is that potential buyers sometimes attend them. When I lecture about pitching, I often ask for volunteers to come to the front of the room so I can coach them on their pitches, and show everyone how these principles can be put into action. I know of many instances where these writers were later approached about their novels or screenplays by agents or editors or producers who heard the writers' "practice" pitches.

Query Letters

Query letters are by far the most common method writers use for getting their material read. If a potential buyer reads a letter that piques her interest, she'll contact the writer and ask to see the material. That, at least, is the theory.

The problem with the theory is that it seldom works that

way, so writers send off bags full of query letters, get no replies and start thinking maybe their parents were right about pursuing a nice, solid career in nursing.

I think the real allure of query letters is not that they're so effective, but that they're so easy. Once a writer composes a good, strong query letter, he can blast it out to every agent in the *Writer's Guide* or the *Hollywood Creative Directory*, then just sit back and wait for the requests to come pouring in. No need to experience the fear, nervousness, frustration and in-your-face rejection of a phone call or pitch fest — the writer can stay where the writer probably wants to stay (or he wouldn't have become a writer): in the safety and solitude of his own home.

Query letters also make life easier for buyers. These never-ending pleas for consideration can be added to the pile of unopened mail, ignored indefinitely, and don't even require a response. If the project sounds like a tough sell, or if the letter is poorly written, it can just be tossed in the circular file. No need to spend hours on the phone taking pitch calls, and no need to experience the discomfort of telling someone to her face that you're not interested in her work.

I'm not criticizing agents and producers and editors for this attitude. As busy as these people truly are, and as bad as most of the projects are that they're approached about, they have very little choice but to establish a policy requiring query letters. But that doesn't mean you, as a writer, shouldn't do whatever you can to get around that policy.

I'm not saying you should avoid sending letters to buyers. But I am saying that these letters work best when you see them as only one part of a process that includes referrals, cold phone calls, pitch fests and competitions. If you regard query letters as a *first step* toward getting your work read, and you tenaciously follow up your letters with phone calls, they can be an essential part of your overall marketing plan.

Below are my basic rules for creating a great query letter. As with any form of writing, simply adhering to the rules isn't enough to make your letter jump off the page; you must add your own particular style and passion and originality. But do so within these parameters:

- *Keep it brief.* Query letters are less than one page long. End of discussion.

- *Make it professional.* This letter is the only evidence a buyer has of your talent, so if you exhibit weak writing skills in composing a simple page, why would he want to read your entire manuscript? Typos, poor grammar, incorrect punctuation, verbosity, a weak style, or a typed or (God forbid) handwritten letter (rather than one printed on business stationery) will result in an immediate pass.

- *Personalize it.* No mail merged, "To Whom It May Concern" letters. Tell the buyer the reason you're writing to *him* regarding your work, rather than to the three hundred other agents or producers you could be contacting.

- *Introduce yourself.* If you have a degree or a background in writing, or in filmmaking, or in the subject matter of your story, say so. Also mention any accolades or achievements you, or your writing, have received (contest prizes, articles, produced plays or screenplays, published novels and short stories, etc.).

  Notice how these last two items match the first steps of your 60-second pitch. First you establish rapport by revealing why you picked this buyer, then revealing something about yourself that increases her interest. You might even include a sentence revealing how you came up with the idea before you segue into your story description.

• *Lead with title and genre.* Unlike your pitch, your query letter should reveal the title of your screenplay, and provide antecedents or demographics, before you describe the story.

It's possible the genre will already be clear, if the reason you gave for contacting this buyer is because they publish or produce or represent projects with the same demographic as yours. If you loved what this buyer said at the Mystery Writers of America convention, it's a safe assumption you've written a crime story.

• *Convey the key emotional beats to the story.* In a single paragraph — two at the most — give a clear picture of what the story is about.

This is where the pitch you've prepared can be of great value. Those key elements of story can be used here as well. In just two or three sentences, it's possible to create empathy for your hero, describe the setup, establish her goal and the obstacles she faces, and reveal any underlying character arc or theme.

Your story description should be more than simply a log line, which is too short and flat to elicit sufficient emotion in written form. But it should also be less than a 60-second pitch, which would take the whole page to write in its entirety. Instead create a powerfully written paragraph that conveys just enough of your story to hook the reader and leave him wanting more.

Let's say you were writing a query letter about our baseball card story from Chapter 2. After revealing why you chose this particular buyer, and mentioning any credits or experience that speak to your writing talent, you might say:

> The Last Mickey Mantle *is a coming-of-age comedy, similar in tone and style to* Stand By Me *and* About a Boy, *about a shy, withdrawn*

ten-year-old boy who, after learning his father is dying, sets out on an odyssey to find the one, priceless item missing from his dad's baseball card collection.

Along the way he's befriended by a con artist who is secretly hoping to get the card for himself. Together they must find and persuade a reclusive billionaire to part with his most valuable possession: Mickey Mantle's rookie baseball card.

If you were to read this and call it a pitch, it would fall flat. It lacks the passion and detail a 60-second pitch possesses. But it gives a clear idea of who the hero is and why we'll care about him, as well as the opportunity, the visible goal, and the inner and outer conflict.

- *No hype.* Same rule as with a pitch. Don't tell the buyer how great or exciting or current or important the story is, and don't proclaim that it will make a fortune, change the world or win a Pulitzer.

- *Promise future contact.* Ask the buyer to contact you if they'd like to see it, but say something like, "*or if you prefer, I will contact you in the next few days to see if you'd like to discuss it further.*"

Even though each query letter you write should be personalized, you can still create a boilerplate, then simply change the opening to match the recipient, keeping a copy of each letter you send.

Emails

The rules for emails are pretty much the same as for query letters. If you can obtain a buyer's email address, I'd recommend using it, since executives often read their own emails, rather than having them screened by assistants. (This is changing, however, as more and more queries come through cyberspace.)

If you send an email, put your letter in the text of the message; many recipients refuse to open attachments which might contain viruses.

Use the same wording as you would for your query letter, but with a simple salutation instead of a date and business address at the top. However, your signoff *should* include your address, phone number and email address, just as your business stationery would.

If you don't get a reply to your email, you can then send the letter as a hard copy, or you can go directly to the follow-up phone call.

Phone Calls

Every agent, every manager, every producer, every publisher and every executive will tell you not to phone them.

I understand. I would too, if I were in their position.

But if I'm a writer with a great screenplay or novel, and I truly believe it can be a hit or a best seller, and if you're an agent or producer or editor whose work I really respect, and if I honestly believe that you'd be an ideal person to be involved in my project and that you'll get richer if you are, then I'm going to do whatever it takes that isn't immoral or illegal or unfairly intrusive to tell you about it. And that includes calling you up.

I won't be rude, I won't be devious, I won't be defensive or gushy or apologetic, I won't take up more than a couple minutes of your time, and I'll talk to an assistant or anyone else at your company if that's what you prefer. But don't ask me not to try.

If you've already written a query letter or an email, follow it up with a phone call a few days later. Ask to speak to the specific person you wrote to, and say that she should be expecting your call. If you already met the buyer at a conference and she told you to call, or if you got a referral from someone the buyer knows, say that.

If this is a cold phone call, do the same thing. You just won't be able to say, "She should be expecting my call."

If the assistant (or whoever you're talking to other than the target person) asks what it's regarding, say that you have a project you want to discuss with this particular buyer.

Here's where it gets tricky, and where most writers cave. If the assistant says, "I'm sorry, but she doesn't accept unsolicited material" or "She's not willing to discuss material over the phone," then reply, "*I understand that's your policy, but ....*" and then explain exactly why you've chosen this buyer to approach with your project. Then say, "*This just seems like such a perfect match for your company, I thought I should call. It will only take two minutes, I promise.*"

Use the phrase "for your company" as a subtle way of including the assistant in the process — to turn him into an ally. If he then says, "I really can't," ask if you can tell *him* about the project. Say, "*I'm pretty sure when you hear about it, you'll want to read it. And once you do, you're going to want to pass it on to your boss.*" Remember, *your goal is to get anyone at the company to read your story.*

Use this same technique if the assistant says he'll have his boss call you back, but she never does. Wait a few days, and if you haven't been contacted, call again. Ask if there's a better time to call to reach the buyer. Or ask if the assistant could schedule a specific time for you to have two minutes on the phone with her.

If the second call isn't returned within a few days, make a third call, only this time say, "*I know how busy your boss is, and I don't want to become a pain in the ass by calling all the time. Suppose I took just 60 seconds to tell you about the project, etc., etc.*"

This approach won't work all the time. In fact, you'll be lucky if it works with one attempt out of every ten. But once your writing and your pitch are ready, you're going to contact dozens of people, and even a 10% success rate — combined with the successes you'll have with all the other approaches — will be enough to get your work in the hands of people who can move it forward.

Elevators

Somewhere along the line, someone described the 60-second pitch as an "elevator pitch," as in, "If you boarded an elevator and Steven Spielberg (for some reason it's always Steven Spielberg who shows up in these fantasy situations) stepped in after you, and pushed the button for the 23rd floor, how would you, in that short amount of time, get him to read your screenplay?"

There is always the possibility — especially if you live in Los Angeles, New York or London — that you'll encounter a possible buyer at a party, or on a bus, or while you're waiting for a restaurant valet to bring your car, or while you're getting *his* car, because you're working as a valet while you finish your screenplay. So you must always have three things with you wherever you go: a well-prepared 60-second pitch; a well-prepared 10-second pitch (see Chapter 10); and a pen and notebook, so that if a buyer expresses interest, you can jot down his contact information.

Two More Opportunities

This is a book about short pitches, not about marketing in general, but I want to mention two other ways of getting your material read: contests and internet listings. Neither of these involves pitching your project, but each one uses the key story and marketing principles we've discussed.

- **Contests.** Writers frequently ask me if writing competitions are worth entering. In my opinion, anything you can do that is legitimate, legal, has proven successful for other writers, and which doesn't surpass your budget, is worth trying. Don't make competitions your only avenue to success — don't make *any* one thing your only avenue — but add them to your marketing arsenal.

Many of the websites mentioned in Chapter 4 have information and links to writing competitions. Look for contests which guarantee that winners will get their work read by as many established producers, publishers or agents as possible. Don't worry so much about prize money — concentrate instead on contests that are less well known, so that you're competing with fewer entries. And see if any regional competitions with added entry requirements apply to you. For example, a contest might insist that your story fall in a certain genre, or that a screenplay take place in the state where the contest is held.

The biggest value of placing in the top three in a competition is that you can include that information in every pitch you make and every query letter you write. It's a great way to increase interest in your project. And every major agency, studio and publisher has staff members who track down contest winners.

- **Internet Listings.** Like pitch fests, log line listings and writers' showcases on sites like *InkTip.com*, *writelink.co.uk*, *screenscripts.com*, *ScriptShark.com*, *scriptpimp.com*, *bookpitch.com*, and *authorlink.com* provide a way for less established writers to get their stories in front of the people in power.

  Every one of these sites claims a high rate of success at getting deals for its members. So before you plunk down your money and put your story out there in front of God and everybody, check them out.

  Go to *donedealpro.com* or *bookwire.com* and search for the titles of the projects listed among a site's success stories. Were they published? Are they in preproduction? Are they listed at all?

If the site reveals the producers or publishers who optioned these projects, look them up in the directories listed in Chapter 4. Then phone the companies directly and ask whoever you can get on the phone if the claim is accurate. Did they find the script or book though the website? Did they truly make a deal? Is it going forward? (And while you have them on the phone, ask what kinds of projects they're looking for now. Always be on the alert for possible places to pitch your own story when it's ready.)

This may sound as if I'm overly skeptical about such sites. I'm actually not — I tend to take them at their word, and consider them worth the effort of pursuing. I just think you should show caution and good judgment about all the places you market your work. Don't pay for the opportunity to be a website's first success story.

Just as I was writing this passage on internet listings, I got a call from a screenwriter who had never heard of such companies. When I mentioned what I was writing about, he said, "If you post your idea on the web, can't somebody steal it?"

This is a question I hear repeatedly. And my answer is always, "Yes, they can. But the only way you can guarantee no one will steal your story is not to show it to anybody. And if that's your approach, what's the point of writing it in the first place?"

Certainly stories do get ripped off. But the work and guilt and legal risk involved in taking someone's log line, developing it into a complete story, writing it, rewriting it, rewriting it again, then marketing and selling it and getting it produced or published without anyone finding out the truth is so great that even for dishonest people, it's almost never worth it.

So protect your material as I describe in Chapter 7, do your best to check out the avenues you pursue, and then get your story out there. What other choice do you have, really?

Finally, if you do use a posting service of some kind, use the principles of telephone pitching to hone your story description into a sentence or two which will captivate the reader, just as you must with your pitch, your log line and your query letter.

PART

II

PRESENTATION

GEARING UP

7

You're almost ready to go. You've got a great story; you've been faithfully researching potential buyers; you've targeted those most appropriate for your project; you've gotten some referrals; you've sent some personalized query letters; and you've registered for a writers conference which includes opportunities for one-on-one sessions.

Now here are a few final thoughts and recommendations before you finally pitch your story.

Protection

Before you send your screenplay or manuscript to anyone — before you even pitch it to anyone or tell anyone your idea — be sure to register it for copyright. (Go to *www.copyright.gov* for information.) This is your best legal protection should someone try to steal your idea.

If it's a screenplay, I'd also recommend registering it with the Writers Guild of America (*wga.org*), though this is credit protection (in case your screenplay is someday rewritten, and the credit issue goes into arbitration), not legal protection. A similar service is offered by the American Screenwriters Association (*www.goasa.com*).

I know lots of lawyers say that copyright is automatic, and that the WGA registration really offers nothing in the way of added protection, so this is all unnecessary. Maybe they're right. But I think it's probably worth the 20 or 40 bucks you're going to spend just to know that someone out there has records that say, "This is yours and yours alone. You did this. It's written down — right here on our official list."

Registering your story is also a nice ritual to mark the completion of your screenplay or manuscript. It officially moves you from the creative stage to the selling stage. That's worth a little money, isn't it?

Clothing

Asking me for fashion advice is like asking a Mormon to recommend a good wine. If my wife didn't buy clothes for me, the only thing I'd ever add to my wardrobe would be socks. Nonetheless, here are my basic suggestions for how to present yourself at a pitch mart:

- **Dress comfortably.** Hollywood is a very casual town unless you're an agent, studio executive, attorney or celebrity on the red carpet. This is especially true for writers. I've seen million-dollar screenwriters show up at meetings looking like they just packed up the sound system for a rock band, then went home and slept in their clothes.

  I don't recommend this particular dress code, but I'd avoid suits, ties, sport coats, dresses and anything else that in most of the country would be regarded as "business attire." You will look overdressed, and perhaps be regarded as trying too hard. Plus pitch fests and conferences involve a lot of walking, standing in lines, leaning on walls and even sitting on floors. Comfort and practicality trumps making a fashion statement.

  New York City, and therefore the publishing world, is a bit more formal, so I'd dress a little less casually going to meetings at a book fair or conference. But stay comfortable. And if you have a meeting in an agent's or editor's office, wear casual business attire.

- **No bare feet.** Even if you're in Hollywood, don't go so casual that you seem like too much of a slob to do a rewrite. Wear shoes and socks. Avoid T-shirts, especially those with writing on them, like the ones that say "U of O Drinking Team" or that list all the stops on the 2003 Simon and Garfunkel tour.

- **No nose rings**. I once heard a pitch from two women who had so many tattoos and piercings I couldn't concentrate on their story. The rule is, if you'd set off an airport metal detector, or if you look like a human graphic novel, you're going to scare the buyer.

- **Don't go topless**. Unless it's important for the integrity of your pitch.

- **Bathe**. Preferably the same day as the pitch fest. And comb your hair.

- **Pop a Tic Tac**. It's hard to revive a pitch when saying the word "Hi" makes your buyer's eyes water.

Props

Story boards, illustrations, toys, weapons and photos of stars who'll be perfect for the parts might add to the emotion of a pitch *meeting*. But be very wary of using anything that will distract your buyer in a 60-second pitch.

If you truly believe that your papier-mâché dinosaur will knock 'em dead, try it out during your rehearsals, and ask your mock buyers if it added to the emotional experience or if it got in the way of your pitch.

Business Cards

Carrying business cards with your name, address, phone number and email address is a good idea, just in case someone you meet — a buyer or a fellow writer — asks, "How can I get in touch with you?"

But I think automatically handing out business cards to everyone you meet at a book fair or pitch fest is a waste of money. If you give one to a buyer during your pitch, what's she going to do with it? Unless she takes the time to write your story points on the back right after your pitch, by the time she gets to her office, there isn't a chance in hell she's going to remember who you were.

I also think cards that say *Writer* or *Author* in the space where your job title goes (or which give the title of your project) are kind of cheesy. One of the few perks of being a writer is that you can *avoid* corporate trappings like long commutes, neckties and pantyhose. So why make it look like you want to give your profession some kind of status by slapping it on a bunch of business cards?

When you've given a successful pitch, follow it up with a professional letter reminding the buyer of your story. This will contain all the information a business card would, but because the buyer receives it at her office, she'll now have something to file, and to remind her who you are.

On-the-Spot Submissions

Don't ever try to hand your manuscript to someone at a pitch fest or conference. Even if he's said yes to reading your book proposal or screenplay, he doesn't want to lug it around for the rest of the day. It's better to mail it to him with a cover letter, as described on page 99, so he'll be reminded of your session, and so you'll have a written record of the submission.

It's okay to have a couple copies of your project with you, on the remote chance that a buyer will *ask* if you have one he can take. If that happens, send him a letter as soon as you're home, reminding him that you gave him the script, and saying how much you look forward to getting his response.

Leave-Behinds

Organizers of pitch fests often ask you to bring synopses of your screenplay to leave with the buyers you pitch to. I hate this idea. I've been reading (and I used to write) synopses and treatments my entire career, and I have yet to encounter one that's emotionally involving. They're a valuable tool for the agents and executives who want summaries of books and scripts, so they can avoid a lot of unnecessary reading time. But synopses are anathema to a novelist or screenwriter. Here's my suggestion. Prepare the best, most powerful synopsis you can of your story. Get coaching or feedback on it just as you would on your other work, to make sure it conveys the emotion of your story as effectively as possible. Make lots of copies, and take them to the conference. But don't offer them to anyone.

Don't even tell the buyer you have one. Instead, make your pitch, and then ask if you can send her the script as outlined on page 99. If she *asks* if you have a synopsis, say, *"Look, there's just no way a synopsis can do justice to my story, or give you a sense of my abilities as a writer. So how about this? Read just the first ten pages. If you're not immediately hooked — and I know you will be — just throw the whole thing away. No harm, no foul."*

Some buyers will be impressed by your confidence and belief in your screenplay, and will agree to do this. Other buyers won't. If they insist on an outline, *then* you can pull out your synopsis and give it to them as requested.

Often you can't avoid leave-behinds, because the person at the pitch fest doesn't have the power to choose what his company will consider. He's been instructed to get synopses of everything he hears, so others at his company can decide which projects they want to see.

Even if you're unwilling to challenge a buyer's synopsis request in the way I've just described, don't ever pull out your synopsis as you begin your pitch. It will lie on the table between you and the buyer, creating a big distraction, and keeping the buyer from total involvement in your story. Instead, give your pitch, then wait for him to request it.

Anathemas

If "anathema" is a noun, shouldn't you say, "A synopsis is *an* anathema to a writer?" Why is it just "anathema"? I mean, you wouldn't say, "Synopsis is problem for writer," or, "Synopsis is pain in ass." Was it once a shorter word, "athema," and when people said "an athema," they kept running it together so it just became one word?

Sorry. I've just always wondered this.

Unnecessary Worries

I've now given you the essential steps for preparing your pitch. But there are additional issues that lots of writers fret about as well. I want to ease your mind about these needless fears:

- **Nervousness.** At the pitch fests I've participated in, you'd think the writers who lined up to pitch their stories were waiting to testify before Congress or get the results of their biopsies. I know pitching your story is a big moment, but it's not going to change your life one way or the other. It's not a once-in-a-lifetime shot — you'll have lots of opportunities to pitch using the methods in this book. Nor does the buyer hold your fate in his hands — there are lots of other agents, producers and publishers looking for stories. And though it may feel otherwise, there are no recorded cases of death by pitching.

  You're going to be nervous. There's really no way around it. It's an unfamiliar situation; the person across the table, or on the other end of the telephone line, does have more power that you do (at least in this particular situation); and it's important to do well to increase the chances of selling your story.

  But here's the big secret about nervousness: *Nobody gives a shit.*

I've heard hundreds of agents and editors and executives talk about the stories and pitches they've heard, and never once has one of them said, "I heard the greatest story the other day. It was exciting and funny and romantic and sexy, and it could make a fortune. But I had to pass because the writer was so nervous."

Nor have I ever heard a buyer say, "The other day somebody pitched me the worst piece of crap I've ever heard. But we went ahead and optioned it because the writer was so *calm*...."

Your buyer wants you to do well. He knows you're nervous, and you have his sympathy. More important, he's desperate for good material. So you can be stuttering, shaking and dripping with sweat, and your buyer will disregard it all if he thinks your story might make him rich.

So instead of worrying about your anxiety, simply allow it. Stop trying *not* to be nervous, and tell yourself, "*Of course I'm nervous — so what?*" Then concentrate on breathing and relaxing as best you can, and focusing on your story instead of on some imagined outcome.

Finally, keep in mind that fear and anxiety are at their peak *before* you begin your pitch. It's the anticipation of what's going to happen that's scary, not the pitch itself. Once you're talking about your project, your focus will be on that, and your nervousness will diminish greatly.

This is why it's so important to get in touch with your passion for the story. Passion is the greatest antidote there is to fear.

• **Performance.** When panelists at conferences talk about great pitches, they often describe some hilarious writer who got a deal because he had them in stitches as he acted out all the characters in his screenplay. Writers hear these stories and think they haven't got a chance because their pitch doesn't play like a *Cirque du Soleil* show.

First of all, these stories are almost always about pitch *meetings*, not 60-second pitches. And I guarantee, no matter how great his dog-and-pony show, no writer ever got a deal in a room unless the buyers had already read his work, and knew he could deliver the goods. More important, performance is not the critical component of a good pitch. *Emotion* is. Some of the best pitches I've ever heard were told very quietly, forcing me to listen more attentively, and pulling me into the story. I don't mean you should mumble or whisper, but you don't have to resort to trumpets and cymbals, either.

As with nervousness, buyers see past attempts to dazzle with style. This isn't *American Idol*. It's your story they'll appreciate, not the way you belt it out.

• **Interruptions**. It's almost a certainty that you'll be interrupted if you're in a full pitch meeting. But it often happens during telephone pitches as well. So prepare for them by rehearsing interruptions when you try out your pitch on friends and family.

During some of your rehearsals, have your mock buyers stop you mid-pitch to pretend to take a phone call. Then when it happens for real, you won't be upset or shaken by it.

When the interruption ends, go back and repeat the last important thing you said before you were stopped. If this means starting over, that's fine. Your pitch is only 60 seconds, so no big deal. Just return to the beginning of the step you'd reached when you were interrupted.

So if it's your acknowledgment that gets interrupted,

repeat that. If you've already revealed how you came up with the idea, then go back to the segue from that into the story: "*So I was just saying that because of my love of baseball cards, I came up with a story about a ten-year-old boy who....*"

Even if the buyer was being rude by taking the other call or listening to his assistant while you were talking, do your best not to let it upset you. And if, after all the interruptions, the buyer passes, be thankful. This inconsiderate person wouldn't be right for your project anyway.

- **Rejection.** As my friend, mentor and father-in-law Art Arthur used to say, "*If you want to be a writer, you've got to reject rejection.*"

  You can't take NO personally, and you can't let it stop you. If a buyer passes, fine. But don't fold up your tent and go home. Just because one person wasn't interested in your story doesn't mean others might not love to read it.

  Discouragement is responsible for as many unpublished novels and unproduced screenplays as bad writing is. You've got to keep dogging away until you find the buyers who respond to you and your material.

  There are a dozen reasons buyers decline to read scripts and book proposals, and a weak pitch is usually far down the list. If a buyer passes, it's probably because she already has a project that's similar in genre or market, or even subject matter and plot. So she has to pass, or she'll end up competing with herself. Similarly, an agent may already represent too many romantic comedy or science fiction or horror writers, and he doesn't want to take on yet another client who'll be up for the same jobs.

A buyer might also have been told by her boss not to consider horror stories, or romance novels, or R-rated films, or women heroes, or any story set in a blue state. You just never know.

I talk more specifically in Chapter 9 about how to respond when a buyer passes. For now I just want to remind you that the more you pitch, the less important any one rejection will be. If your story is truly commercial, you'll find a buyer.

ESTABLISHING RAPPORT

8

S o now, at last, you're face to face — or headset to headset — with your buyer. But before you go diving into the essential elements of your project, you must establish a relationship.

We all want to be in business with people we feel connected to in some way. I've seen or heard of many instances where buyers agreed to read material that sounded commercially weak, but which was presented by people they sensed would be fun or fulfilling to work with.

An agent or executive is more likely to consider your story favorably if she sees you as an individual, not just #14 in the line of people she has to listen to before she can go home.

More important, she'll look upon you much more positively if *she* doesn't feel like she's just buyer #14 on your list of people to pitch to.

The challenge of establishing this kind of rapport with prospective buyers is that you've only got about 15 seconds to do it — and you may not have any idea who they are. But it can be done by using two powerful techniques for introducing yourself.

Common Experience

If you already share something in common with a buyer, you have a big advantage in creating rapport. This is where all that research you did in Chapter 4 will pay off.

If you heard the buyer speak at a writers conference, or Googled her name on the internet, and discovered she graduated from the same college you did, or came from the same home town as you, or used to work as a cab driver just like you did, you have a great way to open your pitch. Simply begin by saying, *"Hi, I'm* [your name] *and I thought it was really cool when you talked about waiting tables while you were breaking into the business. Because that's what I've been doing since I came to LA two years ago."* Or, *"How do you do. My name is* [still your name] *and I've been eager to meet you, because I read that you're a scratch golfer, and I worked my way through school as a caddy at Augusta National."*

You can even follow your introduction up with a related question to engage a buyer more deeply, like, *"Have you ever been to the Masters?"* or, *"Do you have a favorite course here?"* or, *"How do you find time to play, as busy as you are?"* But be careful not to ask something he can't answer in 15 seconds. You don't want to shell out money at a pitch fest and then spend your entire five minutes talking about golf.

You can also link your common experience directly to your story. If you mention that you share your buyer's love of skiing, and that there hasn't been a good ski movie since *Downhill Racer,* because no one has been able to capture both the serenity and the intensity that competitive skiing offers, then you can easily segue into your pitch with, *"and that's what I've tried to do with my screenplay."*

One of the many advantages of referrals is that they provide you with instant commonality. All you have to do is mention the person who recommended you, since you know the buyer has a relationship with her.

Better still, before the pitch, ask your connection if there's anything specific you can mention when you meet the buyer: *"Hi, my name is* [you know who], *and before we begin, Jennifer said to tell you that you owe her a lunch."* (Presumably this friendly message will be light and innocuous. Starting a pitch by saying *"Hi, Jennifer says she knows you're sleeping with her husband"* probably won't lead to a favorable outcome.)

Acknowledgment

Perhaps your most powerful method of creating rapport is by expressing your admiration or gratitude for something the buyer has done. No matter how cold, distant and businesslike a person is, no one is immune from compliments. We all like to hear that what we've done has made a difference to someone.

Again, this is where your research is essential. If you're pitching to a company that produced one of your favorite films, then say that. If you heard your buyer speak, and he enlightened or inspired you, then acknowledge him for that. And if you've admired him for his charitable works, or for something he wrote, or for his reputation for helping newcomers, then those are the things you should open with.

But be specific. Saying, "I loved *Titanic*. Now listen to my pitch," isn't very ingratiating. Saying what you loved about it can be. Think how much more receptive an executive at Lightstorm Entertainment (James Cameron's company) would be if you introduced yourself by saying, "*Hi, my name is* [J.D. Salinger], *and I know you must hear all the time how great* Titanic *was, and how somebody fell in love watching it. But I saw it with my mother. And when it was over, she told me something I never knew — that she had an aunt on the ship who died. And I spent the rest of the night hearing things about my family she'd never told me before. So the movie really means a lot to me.*"

Now, unless you're pitching to James Cameron himself, which is pretty unlikely, the person you're talking to probably wasn't even with the company when the movie was made. But the acknowledgment will still work, because she's representing Lightstorm, and you're acknowledging her company.

These acknowledgments must be sincere, however. Don't say "*The Dukes of Hazzard* changed my life" if it really didn't.

An acknowledgment has an added benefit: It shows a buyer that you've done your homework, and that you specifically chose him to hear your story. You'd be amazed at how few writers expend the little time and energy it takes to research potential buyers, and how many screenwriters just shotgun their scripts to every producer on the *Hollywood Creative Directory* Mailing List CD.

Setting yourself apart as someone who goes the extra distance to get your story produced or published makes you a writer buyers want to work with.

As with common experience, you can also segue from your acknowledgment directly into your story: "*Hi, I'm* [Marcel Proust], *and I read that your agency represents Stephen King. I just want you to know that when I was eleven years old,* The Shining *scared the shit out of me. Ever since, I've wanted to come up with a story that would be that frightening. That's why I was so eager to pitch to you — because I think I finally have.*" And then you launch into the pitch for your horror novel.

If you're contacting a buyer by phone, there's no excuse for not having something to acknowledge her for, or some common experience to mention, because you wouldn't be contacting her if your research or referral hadn't made her a likely candidate for your story.

But at a pitch fest, you will frequently be face to face with buyers you've had no opportunity to research, or who work for companies that haven't made a movie, or published a novel, that you've ever even heard of. So how can you possibly create rapport with them?

Well, if a buyer is listening to you at a pitch mart or conference, he's done at least one thing you should be *deeply* grateful for: He *showed up.*

Sure, it's his job; and sure, he's looking for good material; and of course, his boss made him come. But do you think for one moment he wouldn't rather be spending his Sunday at home with his kids, or watching football, or just catching up on the pile of scripts his boss is also making him read by Monday?

A simple, sincere introduction that says, "*Hi, my name is* [Geoffrey Chaucer], *and before we begin, I just want to thank you for giving up a Sunday to be here. I'm from* [Canterbury], *and it isn't easy to get opportunities to meet people in the publishing world from that far away. So for you to spend your time hearing about my novel really means a lot to me.*"

What editor wouldn't be open to hearing your pitch after receiving an acknowledgment like that?

REVELATION, REQUEST, AND RESPONSE
9

After you've established rapport with your buyer, it's time to reveal your project to her. *Not to tell her your story*, as you know, but to tell her *about* your story in a way that will get her emotionally involved, help her see its commercial potential and make her want to read it.

Awkward Segue #1

One of the deadliest, most awkward moments of your entire pitch session occurs here, right after you've established rapport, when you're ready to launch into the heart of your pitch. You're not sure if you should jump right in, or if you should politely wait for the buyer to ask about your story. If you forge ahead, you risk looking like you're trying to take control of the conversation; if you wait for her go-ahead, and she just sits there, you look like a dolt who forgot why he made the phone call or came to the pitch fest in the first place.

The solution is simple: *Take control.*

This is your time. The buyer has given you the platform, and she wants you to get on with it. Decisiveness is never seen as weakness, and your confidence in your story comes through much more strongly if you boldly begin your pitch.

So after your acknowledgment, or after you've established your common bond with the buyer, let her thank you, then take a single, one-second beat before saying, "*I think the best way to tell you about my story is to tell you how I came up with this idea…*" (or whichever other opening from Chapter 2 you're employing).

Then continue with the pitch you've designed and rehearsed, glancing at your notes occasionally, but mostly looking the buyer in the eye as you talk to her about your project.

The same approach holds true if you're on the telephone, where dead air can be even more uncomfortable than when you're face to face. Establish rapport, take a beat, and then begin revealing your story. Again, don't read your pitch. This is a *conversation* about your story — a conversation that you've carefully prepared, certainly, but also one that is clear, succinct, riveting and fun to hear.

Now all that's left is for you to close the deal. And as any good salesman will tell you, that means *asking for the sale*. In this case, asking the buyer directly if she'll read your screenplay, manuscript or book proposal.

Awkward Segue #2

One of my best friends was once a member of a folk singing group. The group was very good, and they were asked to be on a talent show on one of the Portland, Oregon, television stations.

They were excited about getting to be on TV, and even more excited to learn that their act was going to close the show.

The day of their television debut arrived, their performance went great, and they were feeling terrific… until the host followed their act with his signoff: "Well, ladies and gentlemen, regretfully, that's our show."

I often remember this story when I hear writers' pitches, because most of them end with some version of, "Regretfully, that's my story."

Even more anxiety-provoking than the transition from Rapport to Revelation is the one you must make when you finish describing you story. Because after you've given a powerful, passionate summary of your novel or screenplay, one that you're sure will have the buyer jumping through the phone lines to grab it from your eager hands, you wait for his response. And then…

Nothing.

Silence.

The buyer has no comment at all about your story or your wonderful pitch. So you start to sweat. And squirm. And when you can't take it any longer, you figure you've got to say *something* to make it clear that you're finished, or at least to make sure the buyer didn't hang up or fall asleep while you were talking. So you mumble out something like, "… and … that's all there is." Your terrific pitch turns into what sounds like a meek, uncertain apology, and all of a sudden your story doesn't sound so promising.

The problem is this: The buyer was, in fact, captivated by your pitch, just as you hoped. But when you finished revealing your story, he didn't know for sure if you *were* finished. And he didn't want to be rude and interrupt, in case you had more to say. So he just waited for you to continue. But because you were also waiting for him to respond, nobody said anything, until the silence made you so anxious, you turned into a big, stuttering weenie.

But don't worry. This scenario is never again going to happen to you. Because you're about to learn…

The Win-Win Question

As soon as you've completed the Revelation stage of your pitch by summarizing your story with the log line, you're going to wait one second only. And then you're going to say, *"So, do you have any questions about my story, or would you like me to send you a copy?"*

Look how powerful your pitch has now become. You've offered a succinct, emotional description of the story. You've stayed in charge of the session by following your pitch with a direct question, saving the buyer the awkwardness of wondering if you're finished. You've given him a choice of how to respond without forcing him into a yes or no reply. And whichever way he answers your request, it benefits you.

The subtext of your request is that if he doesn't want to read your story, he must not have heard everything he needs to. So if he simply tells you what isn't yet clear, you'll answer all his questions. And then he's sure to want to read your work.

Once you make your request, and ask your buyer if he has any questions, or if he simply wants a copy, he's going to respond in one of three ways: he'll ask to read it; he'll say no, he's not interested; or he'll ask questions about it.

If the Buyer Says YES

A positive response means you've won. You're done. You got what you came for. Now go away.

The biggest mistake writers make at this point is to keep selling what they've already sold. You wanted the buyer to read your script, and he said he would. What's left to want? For him to read it better? Read it twice? Give you a deal on the spot?

Any additional request — in fact, any additional conversation — can only diminish what you already have, and risks the possibility that the buyer will change his mind, or that you'll undermine the rapport you established by taking up his time unnecessarily.

So all that's left is to thank him, say you look forward to hearing from him, and hang up (if you're on the phone), or leave (if you're face to face).

I know you may not have used the full five minutes you paid for at the pitch fest, but so what? You got what you wanted, and if you excuse yourself early, you've given the buyer a three-minute break he didn't expect. He'll be your friend for life.

After getting your "yes," mail the buyer a copy of the screenplay or manuscript as soon as you can, along with a cover letter reminding him that this is the screenplay he asked to see. Include your log line, making sure it's the same one you used to end your pitch. Don't introduce new story elements that he didn't already hear, and don't try to resell the story in the letter.

If something occurred in the conversation that will nudge the buyer's memory, you can mention that as well: *"I'm the fellow member of the Ann-Margret Fan Club who pitched to you at the EXPO last weekend. As promised, here is* The Last Mickey Mantle, *the screenplay you requested about the ten-year-old boy who has to find the world's rarest baseball card for his dying father."*

Mail or FedEx your submission, keep a copy of the cover letter for your records, and call the buyer's assistant a few days later to make certain it arrived. Then call once a month or so to ask if the buyer has had a chance to read it. Be nice and polite, but be tenacious. It's easy for scripts and manuscripts to get lost in the pile, and perseverance and tenacity always pay off.

If the Buyer Says NO
When a buyer doesn't want to read your script, don't try to change his mind. Either his company isn't interested in the genre or subject matter you've chosen, or they already have a similar project on their development slate, or he knows of a similar project already in the works at one of the studios or publishing houses, or he simply doesn't care about the story.

If you've been pitching to an agent or manager or attorney, a rejection means she doesn't think this is a project she can sell — it doesn't suit her taste, or she has similar projects other clients have written, or it simply isn't playing to her company's strengths and connections.

If this is a telephone pitch, thank the person for her time, and say that you hope you can contact her when your next project is ready to market. Then hang up. Your graciousness and consideration of her time will probably mean as much as the quality of your pitch in encouraging her to take your next call.

If you're at a pitch fest or conference, you have other options in response to a rejection. Since you paid for five, or ten, or fifteen minutes with this buyer, you're entitled to use the rest of your time.

Don't come to the table planning to pitch two stories back to back, and don't tell the buyer you have two projects when you sit down. Pitch the screenplay you believe offers your best shot with this buyer. But if it doesn't turn out to be, take a stab at your second choice by saying, "*I didn't realize you weren't in the market for youth fiction. But I also have a mystery/thriller I've just completed. Would you like to hear about that?*" If you've developed an equally strong pitch for this story, using all the techniques I've presented, it might turn out to be the one she wants to read.

If you've purchased a pitch fest slot and gotten a NO, but you have nothing else to pitch, ask the buyer, "*Since we still have a couple minutes of time left, would you be willing to give me any suggestions on how I could make this a stronger pitch?*" Perhaps you can at least get some free pitch coaching with your remaining time.

After getting the buyer's feedback, you can follow this question with one more: "*Do you know any agencies or production companies* [or publishers] *you think might be more suitable for this story?*" Perhaps you can get a referral, or at least some ideas about the kinds of companies where you should take your story next.

When your time is up, thank the buyer for her input, and say, "*I hope I can contact you when I've completed a script that might be a better match for your company.*" If she says yes (and if you've been professional, gracious and respectful of her time, why wouldn't she?), you can call her office when your next script is ready and honestly tell her assistant that she asked you to call. Even if the person you pitched to is no longer at the company, her previous interest should get you a new agent, editor or executive on the phone.

If the Buyer Has Questions

Questions about your story are a good sign. They show the buyer is interested (or at least polite), and that your desire to get your story read is still alive. Now your answers have to be as succinct and powerful as your pitch was.

The first rule of answering buyers' questions is to *keep it brief*. I've heard writers give superb pitches, religiously sticking to their 60-second limit, and then use a simple question as an excuse to do the unthinkable: *Tell their story*. If your answer to any question lasts more than ten seconds, then you didn't rehearse enough, or you didn't listen carefully to the question.

Listening is as important a part of pitching as preparing, and is probably harder. You're relieved to have finished your pitch, you're anxious about getting a yes, and you're thinking more about the buyer's opinion of you than about what he wants to know.

So if our baseball card story elicited the question, "How does he find the card?" a good answer would not begin, "Well, when the movie opens, we see some old newsreel footage of Mickey Mantle hitting a home run, and then...."

A far better answer would be, "*He goes online and learns that the three remaining cards belong to a notoriously underhanded collector, a retired baseball player and a reclusive billionaire. So he sneaks on a train and heads off to find them one by one.*"

It's of course possible this buyer was asking for more detail, such as "Which one does he persuade?" or "How does he finally get the card?" or "Does he try to steal the card from the billionaire?" But if he wants more information, he'll ask, and you can take another ten seconds to answer.

This is a far better approach than spending two of your precious minutes offering a lot of unnecessary detail, when the only thing the buyer wants to know is your hero's age.

I think the reason it's so difficult to come up with succinct answers is because we tend to believe that if a buyer has questions, they didn't understand our story at all. So we want to say, "No, you don't get it! Just listen to my whole story and you'll see how great it is!"

But they do get it. Almost every buyer you meet has worked on hundreds of novels or screenplays before they ever hear your wonderful pitch. So give them credit for anticipating the beats of your story, and staying ahead of you as you reveal them. Their questions are to help them clarify either the kind of book or movie this will be (the specific genre and market), and the elements that make your particular story unique. Short, simple answers will do that far better than long, drawn out details.

Sometimes buyers' questions take the form of suggestions; they offer ideas for how to make your story stronger or more commercial. This is also a good sign, as it means they're already thinking about how to reach an audience with your story. Your best response is to consider every idea they have, and come up with ways that will make them work.

I realize this isn't easy. You've spent a big chunk of your life perfecting your precious creation, and now some lowly underling stuck at a pitch fest thinks he's going to tell you to change it — and make you do all the work. Your natural reaction will be to get defensive and protective of your story, and reject any suggestions, especially those requiring a major rewrite.

But saying no to the buyers' ideas doesn't get you anywhere. And you're not committing to anything, you're just brainstorming along with them as they suggest new ideas for your story. If it keeps them interested, why not play along? Remember, your goal is to get them to read it, and by the time they do, they'll have probably forgotten whatever suggestions they made at the pitch fest.

And there's always the possibility they're right. Hard as it might be to accept, one of the positive results of pitching your story to a lot of buyers is that you'll get a number of suggestions that you can incorporate whenever you begin your next rewrite. And if you consistently hear the same concerns or suggestions, go back to the drawing board and address these weaknesses before you continue pitching your story.

Often the best response to a buyer's idea is with questions of your own. Rather than agree or disagree with his suggestion, try to clarify why he's making it. If you understand his reasoning, you can suggest an alternate solution to his concerns that doesn't destroy the parts of your story you love most.

So if a buyer suggested *The Last Mickey Mantle* would be better with a girl as the hero, you wouldn't say, "Are you nuts? Girls don't collect baseball cards!" Instead you might ask, "*Do you think that would make the hero more sympathetic, or is it because a girl would be a stronger draw for the tweener market?*" If that, in fact, is his underlying concern, you can say, "Maybe we could introduce a girl into the story that would help him find the card. That would increase the demographic, and still keep the story credible, since most card collectors are boys."

Sometimes buyers will get so involved in your story that you exceed the five minutes you promised the phone call would last. (This won't happen at a pitch fest; they have big, burly bouncers who will drag you out of your chair when your time is up.) But if your 60-second pitch goes long because the *buyer* keeps talking, that's fine. She's responsible for her own time, and you should keep responding to her ideas and questions. Just make certain you're not the one prolonging the conversation.

Once you've answered your buyer's question(s), don't allow that awkward silence to reappear. Restate your request: "*So, do you have any more questions, or do you think this is a project your company would be interested in?*" If she still has more questions, just keep the process going until she agrees to read your story.

10

This book has focused on pitching your own novel or screenplay. But what if your story is nonfiction? What if you're pitching a TV series, or a reality show, or a how-to book? What if you're a producer trying to get a financier to read a script you've optioned? Or a reader or development executive at a publishing house or production company, having to pitch a story you just read?

Perhaps most important, what if you don't even have 60 seconds, and you have to pitch your story in an instant?

With some modification, the process I've outlined will apply to all these situations.

The 10-Second Pitch

As soon as you begin telling people that you've written a book or screenplay, the question you'll get over and over is, "What's it about?"

If you hear these words sitting across from a buyer, you know it's an invitation to begin your pitch. But if you're at a party, or if you meet an agent in the hotel lobby at a writers conference, or in almost any situation not specifically designed for pitching, the person asking doesn't want a sales pitch, and he doesn't want to listen for a full minute or more while you try to persuade him to read your story. He doesn't want you to persuade him to do anything. He's just curious and polite.

This doesn't mean you don't want to be prepared with the most powerful description of your story possible. A great 10-second "pitch" will pique people's interest, will often get them asking questions, and might sometimes get your story read.

So as soon as your story is ready to talk about, spend time preparing this short description so it's as emotionally compelling as possible.

Begin with the same list of ten key story elements, then pare it down to the three or four most powerful. In most cases, this means focusing on Hero, Desire and Conflict, plus the one additional element that makes the story unique.

Let's say you were writing the screenplay *Kingdom of Heaven*. You might say, "*Well, I've always loved the stories of the Crusades. So I'm writing about a single young knight who saves an entire city during a huge battle between the Christian and Muslim armies.*"

Obviously — at least I hope it's obvious by now — this would not be a good pitch. It doesn't pull us into the story, or tell us enough about the hero, or mention the love story, or even reveal which side he's on.

But if you only have ten seconds or so, it has enough conflict and emotion to stimulate further discussion if the person you're addressing is interested. It reveals the basic setting, the hero, his visible desire and the major conflict. And the opening adds one other element — your passion for the story (or at least for the historical backdrop).

If you were the author or screenwriter of *Brokeback Mountain* and someone said "What are you writing?" you might answer, "*Actually, it's a classic, tragic love story set in the early sixties, about two people who meet in the harsh Wyoming wilderness and want nothing more than to be together, but who can't, because they're both men.*"

This single sentence does nothing to convey the power, or complexity, or passion of the novella or the screenplay or the film. But by beginning with the setup, genre, heroes and desire, this short pitch at least creates expectations that are shattered when the conflict is revealed, and this surprise will stimulate interest in the specific elements of the story.

Here are some additional principles and suggestions for preparing a 10-second pitch:

- **Don't reveal your story until you're ready.** Your stories are your creations, and an idea revealed too soon is like a child taken from the womb prematurely. It isn't strong enough to withstand the harsh elements of the outside world. If you are in the early stages of formulating your story (unless you're working with a consultant, or in a class designed specifically to help you develop it), keep it to yourself.

  If someone asks you what you're working on, be vague: *"I've got a lot of ideas right now and I haven't picked one yet"* or *"I'm just getting started and I'm not really ready to talk about it."* If you prefer, just make up some idea you never plan to write, or tell people you're still working on your last script, which you actually finished a month before. Otherwise they might offer suggestions or criticism which will overwhelm or depress you.

- **A 10-second pitch is not a log line.** Though they obviously have much in common — brevity, hero, desire, conflict — a pitch is verbal, and should be more casual, and presented with more passion and emotion. A log line might read, *"The lives of a dozen strangers all intertwine — sometimes violently and sometimes courageously — against a backdrop of crime and racism in Los Angeles."* But if you asked Paul Haggis and Bobby Moresco what their screenplay *Crash* was about, and they answered with that sentence, you'd think they were robots — or that they were reading their log line.

- **Empty lead-ins are okay.** It's pretty awkward to jump right into your prepared pitch without sounding like you just pulled it out of a can. That's why the two short pitches above began, "Well, I've always…" and "Actually, it's…." You need some meaningless segue to maintain the sense that this is a conversation, not a speech.

- **"*What if?*" can be just as powerful as in a full pitch.** Revealing how you came up with an idea can be an effective lead-in even when you've only got ten seconds. Suppose you'd written *The 40-Year Old Virgin*. When asked about your new script, you might answer, "*You know how there have been a bunch of comedies like* American Pie *or* Fast Times at Ridgemont High, *about high school kids losing their virginity? Well, what if the virgin was a 40-year old man?*"

Pitch Meetings

At the other end of the pitching spectrum is the full pitch meeting, which is at least 15 minutes long, and can sometimes last an hour or more (not because you came in with a one-hour pitch, but because of your interaction with the buyers).

As I said in the introduction, this book doesn't focus on pitch meetings; there are several other books on the market that go into great detail about what to do when you have so much time with a buyer. And pitch meetings rarely occur in the book world — your proposal will speak for itself. But if you're a screenwriter, I do have some thoughts and suggestions about applying the principles of the 60-second pitch to its longer counterpart.

- **Use the 10 key elements to prepare your long pitch.** No matter how long your presentation, you want to focus on the most emotional elements of your story. And with the time afforded you in a pitch meeting, you should be able to incorporate all ten items on the list in Chapter 1 (with the possible exception of character arc and deeper issues, if those don't apply).
- **Open with your short pitch.** Just as at a conference or

on the telephone, the 60-second pitch can access your passion, draw the buyer into the story and leave her wanting more, which you will then provide in the full pitch.

Opening with a one-minute pitch also gives the buyer a clear idea of exactly what she's about to hear, so she doesn't spend half the meeting trying to figure out the genre, or where the story is headed. And a short pitch doesn't give away the ending, so she'll still be anticipating how the story might turn out.

Sometimes when you begin this way, a buyer will say, "Oh, I didn't realize this was a heist movie. We already have two of those in development, and I'm afraid we won't be interested, no matter how good the story is." Having your carefully prepared, 45-minute pitch shut down after two minutes might sound horribly depressing. But wouldn't you prefer to find out right away — rather than *after* you've been there an hour — that the entire meeting is pointless?

And of course, a meeting is never really pointless — you can still establish rapport and impress buyers with your passion and professionalism, which will make them eager to hear your next project.

• **Announce your progress**. Unlike a telephone pitch, in a pitch meeting you *are* trying to tell your story, with enough details and beats to show that the concept is thoroughly developed. But because this makes your pitch so long, you want to announce the key turning points when you reach them, so the buyer will know just how far into the story you've gone, and how much is left. Phrases like "At the end of Act 1…" or "Right at the midpoint of the movie…" are welcome.

When I worked in development, I once sat through a pitch that seemed endless. Finally, when the writer got to what I thought must be the climax, he announced, "And then at page 10...." Not a successful meeting, I'm afraid.

- **Don't try to tell your whole story.** I know that a pitch meeting is designed to reveal the full story for your screenplay, but that doesn't mean you talk about every scene. Brevity is always valued in Hollywood, and hitting the major beats of story and character is far more important than describing every single scene.

  A buyer wants to know that you've worked everything out in a compelling way, that the story is commercial and that the character arcs, themes and emotions will come through clearly. If he wants to hear all the dialogue and experience all the action and characters, he'll wait and read the screenplay.

Pitching Episodic Television

I'm a little reluctant to talk about this, because if you're trying to launch your career as a TV writer, you won't do it by creating an original sitcom or one-hour series. With very rare exceptions, the episodic series that make it to the screen are created by well established producers — screenwriters who have worked their way up the ladder from spec writer to assignment writer to staff writer to producer to executive producer, and even to show runner. So unless you've made that journey, I strongly suggest — and so does every other agent or TV writer I've ever encountered — that you keep writing sample episodes of current, successful series, until you actually get paid to write one.

In spite of the fact that this advice is given again and again and again, writers keep thinking they're the exceptions. And maybe you are. Maybe you have a published novel that's been successful, and they're letting you pitch the series as a means of acquiring the rights. Maybe you have a friend who is established, and has said he'll partner up with you if you come up with a good idea. Maybe somebody's even come along who just says, "I don't care if you've got a track record. If it's a good story, I'm interested."

If so, be sure your material is well protected, and be aware they may just want to buy the idea from you, leaving you with very little cash, and no credit at all. If you still want to take your shot, use all the same pitching principles I've outlined, modified to meet the needs of a series.

In episodic series, what's most important is that:

- **The arena is enticing.** It can be a law firm, a crime scene unit, a dysfunctional family, an office, an apartment building, a neighborhood, a mysterious island or a town after an alien invasion. But it must be intriguing or inviting in some way, and it must present lots of opportunities for conflict.

- **The characters are compelling.** The people who populate your story must be interesting, empathetic and varied enough that audiences will want to see them week after week.

- **The conflict is emotionally involving.** The obstacles the characters face must be great enough that it will be possible to come up with a hundred episodes if the show's a success.

When hearing an idea for a new television series, buyers want to know exactly where it will fit on the TV schedule: which network; which time slot; which demographic. So use successful antecedents. If there's anything resembling a clone factory in Hollywood, it's the world of episodic television. (Or is it just a coincidence that when *CSI: Crime Scene Investigation* premiered, it was the only show on television portraying forensic science — or reenacting crimes in flashback as evidence was found — and two seasons later there were about 85 shows doing the same thing?)

Follow your overall description of the series with a pitch of the pilot: the episode that will establish empathy with the characters and reveal how they got into the situation they'll remain in for the rest of time.

Focus on the central character of the series in your pilot, even if eventually all the main characters will be heroes of some of the episodes. And make sure your pitch reveals the characters' inner conflicts and the deeper themes the show will explore.

Series characters don't have arcs the way novel and movie characters do, because their flaws and weaknesses will recur in different ways week after week.

For ten years, every episode of *Friends* touched on the same theme: the struggle to move from dependence on family and friends to self-reliance and responsibility. Repeatedly the series got humor and emotion out of Monica's competitiveness and obsession with neatness, or Chandler's low self esteem and defensive humor, or Joey's womanizing and level of intelligence.

And no matter what drove a particular story line of *The West Wing*, every episode portrayed the conflict between idealism and political pragmatism — in addition to whatever inner conflicts each character consistently revealed. These are the kinds of qualities you must convey when you pitch a series concept.

If you are making your way up the episodic television ladder, it's far more likely that you'll be invited to pitch an episode for an existing series. This opportunity arises after the staff writers and producers of a series have seen one or two of your sample episodic scripts — usually for competing shows — and they like your writing enough to want to meet with you.

This is a pitch meeting, not a 60-second pitch, since no producer would ever listen to ideas for an existing show over the phone or at a pitch fest. But again, many of the same principles apply, with modification.

When pitching an episode, you don't need to introduce, or create empathy for, the hero, since the audience already knows that character. Just don't come up with an episode where an outside character enters the regular characters' lives and then drives the story. TV series are always about the stars.

Focus on one or more of the regular characters' desires and conflicts. These will be different each week, and getting the job depends a great deal on how original and funny — or dramatic — your idea is. Before you develop the idea, go to *www.tv.com* to see descriptions of every previous episode in the show's history. Then create one that hasn't been done before.

Whatever the hero's goal in your pitch, it must be consistent with the character that has already been established, and should grow out of traits and flaws we're already familiar with. Over the course of a series, things do change: characters die, get married, get their own spin-offs. But don't let life-changing events occur to the regular characters in your episode. The buyer wants to know that you understand the rules of the series, and will maintain the status quo.

Some story elements, like the setup and the antecedents, won't apply to a TV series pitch. But you still want to establish rapport with the buyers, and you'll still convey your passion, both for the series and for your original episode.

Pitching Everything Else

What if you want to make a deal for a reality show, or a game show, or a talk show, or a documentary, or a nonfiction book, or a self-help book, or a music video, or a grand opera, or a school play? It really doesn't matter — everything's built on story. Just use the process I've outlined as a jumping off point, then modify it to convey the emotional power of your project.

If it's a documentary or nonfiction book, focus on the individuals who will be at the center of the story. I bet even Michael Moore would agree that much of the power of *Fahrenheit 911* came from his portrayal of a conservative, patriotic mother whose son died in battle, and how the tragedy shifted her consciousness. If you were pitching that project, it's the kind of detail you'd want to include along with all the larger political and moral issues the film raises.

The same holds true if it's a historical book or documentary. Obviously biographies require you to pitch those elements of the subjects' lives that make them empathetic and convey their greatest conflicts and highest achievements. But even the most sweeping, far-reaching historical subjects rely on individual stories. If you can personalize the grandness of your book or film in this way, your pitch will be stronger, and the likelihood of a deal much greater.

Imagine beginning your pitch like this: "*As you probably know, the greatest loss of American life in battle wasn't Iraq, or Vietnam, or even World War II; it was the Civil War. But in the midst of one of the bloodiest battles of that horrific conflict, a young officer who knew he would probably die the next day created one of the most beautiful love letters ever written. After another battle, a Confederate woman whose husband was away at war turned her plantation into a hospital, and saved the lives of more than eight hundred men. I want to do a 14-hour television documentary that reveals 50 more unheard stories like these, along with all the political, social and historical forces that led to one of the defining events in our nation's history.*"

I'm sure Ken Burns had a better pitch than that when he raised financing for *The Civil War*. He may not have had to pitch it at all — I mean, he is Ken Burns. But it's not hard to imagine that a pitch like that would pique a buyer's interest, and make her ask for more.

Even if your documentary doesn't have a human being in sight — if it's a nature film like *March of the Penguins* — you can still anthropomorphize your subjects enough to give a sense of the conflicts they face, and the connection to them we will feel. The essential principles of story remain the same.

And if your book is an instructional or self-help book, get the manuscript or proposal read by focusing on the people it will benefit, rather than the specific steps it outlines to achieve wealth, or health, or happiness, or beauty, or a perfect golf swing. Every instructional book ever written was created to solve a problem: lack of knowledge; lack of skill; a need for inspiration; a desire to have something more. But problems mean conflict, and conflict elicits emotion, and emotion creates connection, and connection means sales.

Pitch your book proposal using anecdotes that create empathy between the publisher or agent and the book's potential audience. Get your buyer to root for your readers' success, and convince that buyer that there are thousands of those potential readers out there, just waiting for their lives to be changed.

Regardless of what you're pitching, buyers — and readers — want to be drawn into the world you've created. We want to know who we're rooting for, what those characters want, and what makes their desires seem impossible. We want to know why you think this will appeal to lots of people. And we want to feel your passion for your project.

Marketing Other People's Stories
I assume most of you reading this book are writers. But what if you're a producer or director or agent or manager or development executive or reader, trying to get someone to read

something authored by someone else? Do all the principles outlined in this book apply to you as well?

You know they do. Otherwise I wouldn't ask the question.

If you're on the phone hoping to make an eventual sale — if you represent a writer, or if you own the film rights to a book or screenplay — the telephone pitch is exactly the same as it would be if you'd written the story yourself. But instead of beginning, "Let me tell you how I came up with this idea," open with, "*I think the best way to tell you about this project is to tell you what I love about it.*" And then tell your buyer exactly that.

You actually have a big advantage pitching something not your own — you can hype it. If a writer says her script is hilarious, and will make a fortune, the buyer immediately assumes it's not, and it won't. You know this is true, because if you're reading this part of the book, you *are* a buyer of some kind, and it's exactly what you think when you hear a writer say those words.

But if you tell someone else a book or screenplay is hilarious, they'll probably believe you. At least they'll believe that you *think* it is. And because you like the project enough to invest your time, your reputation and perhaps your money to get it published or produced, the buyer figures it's got a better shot than the average book or screenplay.

Don't say a story you represent is brilliant or commercial or great if you don't truly believe it is. Just say what you honestly think of it. If you're just bullshitting for the sake of a client, tell the client he needs to keep rewriting, and work with him until you do love it. Then take it out.

If you start hyping stuff dishonestly, it's going to be harder and harder to get buyers to read the stuff that really is great, when it finally comes along.

Pitching to Your Boss

If you're pitching your boss instead of a buyer, I recommend you use the 60-second pitch, *whether you like the story or not.* Here's why:

Let's say you're participating in the dreaded Monday Morning Meeting. This is the weekly ritual at most agencies or studios or publishing houses where everyone talks about the stuff they read that weekend, and suggest which projects are worth considering for representation or production or publication.

When the turn rolls around to you, you've got to sound interesting, even though 12 other stories have already been discussed, and everyone's eyes are starting to glaze over. The 60-second pitch is invaluable in this situation.

People in power — especially the heads of agencies and production companies — never have time to spare. Neither do publishers and book agents. They all want to hear only what they need to know to make a decision, and then move on. If you can avoid trying to tell the story, and can keep each "pitch" to less than a minute, I guarantee you'll be the rising star of the company.

Come to the meeting prepared. Work from notes, not from memory. And never, ever read your presentation aloud.

Begin with what you love about the story, or what real life situation or previous movie you believe might have led the writer to create it. Convey the most important of the list of ten elements, especially the antecedents. End with the log line, and then stop briefly, allowing anyone to jump in with questions.

Then weigh in with your opinions. This way your boss knows she heard a strong, objective presentation of the best the story has to offer. If, after giving a strong pitch, you say you thought it was poorly written, or the characters were one-dimensional, or the story was too familiar, or you don't think it's right for the company, you aren't preventing your boss, or anyone else, from suggesting that it might still be worth considering.

The reason I suggest pitching everything as if it's your own is to give your associates as clear an idea as you can of the potential of the story. If you open by saying the script was crapola, and you then go on to say it was about this guy who blah, blah, blah, you've reduced your effectiveness. Your boss can't express any interest at all without contradicting you, which will make at least one of you look bad. She won't even be sure she heard what she needed in order to make a decision, since everything you said was colored by your dislike of the material.

If your rejection of a story is based on some subjective reaction you have to religious themes or period pieces or horror stories or romance novels, then the company might end up passing on something with commercial potential. And if you open by gushing about how great the story is, and it's of no interest to anyone else at the table, you look like you don't fit in. Either way, your job promotion just got pushed further into the future.

There's one additional reason to pitch everything with objectivity and passion. It's more enjoyable for everyone. Stories well told — even in 60 seconds — are fun to hear. And fun to present. So your short, well-designed pitch will make everyone feel good. And make you look good.

PART

III

EXTRA STUFF

THE PITCHING TEMPLATES
11

T he following templates are designed to give you a very clear understanding of how the principles of the telephone pitch can be applied to a variety of situations. You should be able to put the details of your story into one of these models, and use it as a foundation for creating your own powerful pitch.

But I beg you; please use these as a *starting point*. Don't just plug in your story, print it out, and call that your pitch.

First of all, if everyone who reads this book does that — and I fully expect those people to number in the millions — then a lot of publishers, filmmakers and agents are going to hear the same pitch over and over again.

More important, a fill-in-the-blank approach won't make the pitch your own. It'll have none of your personality or passion, and it won't allow for the changes you must make to convey the emotional power of your particular story.

When I coach writers and filmmakers on their pitches, I always employ the principles I've presented in this book. But I begin by asking lots of questions about the story, so I have a real sense of where the idea came from, and where the client's passion lies. What was it about the story that prompted my client to commit at least a year of his or her life to getting it onto the page or up on the screen?

You must follow the same process for yourself. Get a clear sense of why the story just *has* to be published or produced, and insert those qualities into the templates below in a way that reflects your own voice, your own story and your own passion.

And a word of warning: If you just jumped ahead to this chapter for an easy shortcut to a good pitch, it's not going to work. It's not even going to make sense unless you've read through the whole process first.

As you will see, the elements of the templates can be interchanged quite easily. I've simply combined a variety of lead-ins, segues and story elements to provide lots of possibilities. So if you like, combine the opening from one template with the antecedent reference of another, add the love story description or thematic statement from two more, and create your own pitch that way. As long as it gets buyers emotionally involved, gives them a clear sense of what they're going to read, convinces them of your project's commercial potential, and conveys your passion, it'll be great.

These templates assume you've already established rapport with the buyer, and are now ready to begin the revelation part of your pitch.

| The Genre Film Template | I think the best way for me to begin is to tell you how I came up with this idea. I've always been a huge fan of [**genre of your film or novel**], especially ones like [**antecedent #1**] and [**antecedent #2**], or even [**antecedent #3**], where [**the thing that these antecedents have in common with your story, which sets them apart from others in the genre**]. But in most of those stories, [**the plot element that's true for the antecedents, but not for your story**].

So I started thinking, "What if [**the thing that sets your story apart from your antecedents, and makes it unique**]?" And that's certainly true of [**hero's name**], the hero of my [**screenplay or novel**], [**title**]. He's a [**age**]-year old [**occupation**] who's [**setup, source of empathy**]. But when [**opportunity**], he decides/has to [**new situation**]. So he sets out to [**outer motivation**] by [**plan to accomplish his goal**].

The only problem is [**outer conflict, or complication that makes the obvious conflict even greater**], so now he has to [**only remaining way to accomplish the goal, which seems impossible**]. So [**title**] is a story about [**log line**]. |

Before I get into the story, I should tell you that when I was [age] I [your situation at that time]. And then I [personal experience that connects you to your idea]. So I started thinking, "What if [basic premise of your story]?" And that's just what happens in [title]. [Hero's name] is [qualities for empathy], until [situation that links your hero to your "What if...?"] So now [hero's name] must [outer motivation] before [outer conflict or ticking clock]. And the only way she can do that is by overcoming her fear of [inner conflict] and [plan that evolves, which seems impossible to accomplish]. So this is ultimately a story about [log line], which explores [deeper issues], and says that [universal theme].

The Personal Experience/ Fictional Story Template

Let me begin by saying I've always been a huge fan of [genre of your film or novel], especially ones like [antecedent #1] and [antecedent #2], or even [antecedent #3], where [the thing that these antecedents have in common with your story, which sets them apart from others in the genre]. Well, when I was [age] I [your situation at that time]. And then I [personal experience that connects you to your idea].

So I started thinking, "What if [thing that unites your antecedents with your personal experience, to make your story unique]?" And that's how I came up with the idea for [title]. My hero is a [age]-year old [occupation] who's [setup, source of empathy]. But when [opportunity], he decides/has to [new situation]. So he sets out to [outer motivation] by [plan to accomplish his goal].

The only problem is [outer conflict, or complication that makes the obvious conflict even greater], so now he has to [only remaining way to accomplish the goal, which makes it seem impossible]. So this is a story about [log line].

The Combined Personal Experience/ Fictional Story and Genre Template

The Real Situation/ Fictional Story Template	I don't know if you're aware of this, but [real situation you became aware of]. So I wanted to explore what would happen if a [description of your hero] who [setup/empathy] was all of a sudden [opportunity]. So now she's determined/forced to [outer motivation] so she can [why the hero thinks this goal will lead to self worth]. The problem is, she is unaware that [outer conflict], which will force her to face her fear of [emotional fear] in order to ultimately [hero's arc or transformation] and be able to [finish line/visible representation of outer motivation].
The Love Story Template	[Use any of the openings above up to the point in your story where your love interest is introduced. Then say:] So my story is about [hero's name], a [role/empathy/setup] who wants to [outer motivation other than the love story]. But then my hero falls in love with a [romance character's occupation], who is [quality that links the romance character to the original outer motivation]. So now my hero has to overcome [conflict that makes the original goal difficult], while [conflict that intertwines the love story with the original outer motivation, making it now seem impossible to win everything]. So [title] is a romantic [genre you've added the love story to] like [antecedent #1] or [antecedent #2], about a [description of hero] who has to [outer motivation] and win the love of [description of romance character].

One of the reasons I've been so eager to tell you about my story is that I was a huge fan of [antecedent the buyer produced, published or represented], because I love stories where [quality their antecedent shares with your story]. Well imagine what would happen if a [setup that creates empathy with your hero] discovered that [opportunity], and now the only hope of [outer motivation] is if he can [seemingly impossible plan to achieve that goal]. And while [specific steps to plan], he [major setback that makes it seem like all is lost].

Now what if I told you that this actually happened, in [year of true story], when [real person] had to [real accomplishment], and [what real person did, which you haven't mentioned already]. And now I have the rights to that story, and that's what my [screenplay/novel] is about.

The True Story Template

Two Sample Template Pitches

To illustrate how these templates can be put to use, here is a possible pitch for Bob Fisher and Steve Faber's screenplay *Wedding Crashers*.

Notice that I've used elements of the Genre Film Template and the Real Situation/Fictional Story Template and then added the love story template. I also modified some of the individual elements of those templates, so my pitch would best fit this particular story. But this should give you an idea of how filling in appropriate blanks can give you a good starting point for designing your own 60-second pitch.

I think the best way for me to begin is to tell you how I came up with this idea. I've always been a huge fan of Romantic Comedies, especially ones like Hitch *or* Working Girl *or even* There's Something About Mary, *where the hero has to lie about who he truly is to get what he wants.*

Then one day I read about these guys who would crash big weddings where they didn't even know the bride or groom, just to get free food and booze, and to pick up women. So I started thinking, "What if two commitment–phobic party animals who were master bullshit artists found out that the daughter of some rich, highly protected government official was getting married?" And that's how I came up with Wedding Crashers, *a story about two womanizers who want to crash the biggest, most exclusive wedding imaginable.*

But then each of them falls in love with one of the bride's sisters. So now they must maintain their fictional identities as big business moguls while overcoming a gay, psychotic brother, a nymphomaniac mother, an obnoxious fiancée, a protective father and their fears of commitment and responsibility, all the while keeping the women they love from learning the truth.

Here's a second example, this one for Gary Ross and Anne Spielberg's screenplay *Big*, which uses the combined Personal Experience/Fictional Story and Genre Template, then adds elements of the Love Story template:

Let me begin by saying I've always been a huge fan of fantasy comedies, especially ones like Liar Liar *and* The Nutty Professor, *or even* Bruce Almighty, *where a character makes some kind of wish, or declaration, or just longs for some impossible thing, thinking it's the answer to all his problems, and it turns out to be a curse to overcome.*

Well, when I was in junior high, I was very short for my age. And I always wished I could be big like the cool kids.

So I started thinking, "What if a kid actually got that wish, and it gave him the body of a 30-year-old man?" And that's how I came up with the idea for Big.

My hero is Josh, a 12-year-old boy who's so short he can't even get on the cool rides at a carnival. But when he puts a coin

in a fortune-telling machine and wishes he was big, he wak
the next day and discovers he's got the body of a 30-year-old
No one except his best friend believes what happened —
think Josh is missing — so he decides to move to New York City
and pretend he really is 30 until he can find the fortune telling
machine and wish himself back to his normal, 12-year-old body.

To survive in New York, he gets a job with a toy company,
where he's brilliant, because he actually still plays with toys. But
then my hero falls in love with a co-worker at the toy company,
who is going to help him design a toy of his own. So now my
hero has to overcome all the problems of being an adult when he
only has the intelligence and experience of a 12-year-old, while
ultimately having to choose whether to stay a grownup and give
up his childhood, or to make another wish and go back to who he
was, and give up the woman he loves.

Again, notice that I didn't follow the two templates
exactly — Big is less about *winning* the romance character's
love than *sustaining the relationship* in spite of his secret. You
will always have to use your own judgment in this way,
and mold the templates to fit the needs of your stories.

Out of curiosity, I contacted Bob Fisher, one of the
writers of *Wedding Crashers*, to see if in fact the deal for the
movie was made because of a pitch. It was.

It actually came out of a half-hour pitch meeting, but
Bob said he and Steve Faber began the pitch with the hook,
saying, "*It's easy to meet women at weddings, so these guys think,*
'Why just go to the two weddings a year you get invited to?' So
they decide to crash weddings." In other words, they opened
their pitch by revealing how they came up with the idea.

Bob also said they were able to get that meeting — and
meetings at all the studios — because a lot of people read and
loved a spec screenplay of theirs which had already been
optioned. They were able to get *that* spec screenplay read

because they had been very successful television writers. And they launched their television career by persuading lots of people to read their spec TV scripts.

See how it all comes together when you start with a great story, and a great pitch?

"The Best Pitch I Ever Heard"
EXECUTIVES ON PITCHING
———— 12 ————

Rather than limit this book to my own opinions and advice about 60-second pitches, I asked a lot of other people in power about what *they* look for in a good pitch. Below are their responses.

The contributors include agents, producers, publishers, attorneys, managers, development executives and writers from the US, England, and Europe. All of them have been on the receiving end of lots and lots of pitches.

The insights these generous contributors offer are outstanding and varied. Some are broad and general, some are very specific. Some address novels, some screenplays and TV episodes. Some are inspiring, some cautionary. Most pertain to short pitches, but some focus on longer pitch meetings. But all of these insights will give you additional information, ideas and guidance in creating and presenting your pitches.

And if you ever find yourself pitching to one of these people, you'll know what they look for, and you'll have a great basis for acknowledgment.

I thought about adding some comments of my own throughout the chapter to emphasize or expand on what these experts say. Or maybe to gloat when a top buyer agrees with something I said earlier in this book (it's the sophisticated, literary version of "*Told ya, told ya!*"). But I decided to let everyone's comments stand on their own.

Just a couple things I want you to notice as you read through all of these ideas.

Again and again, the comment you will hear repeated is that weak pitches have too many details. This simply reinforces the #1 rule I've been preaching through this entire book: *Don't try to tell your story.*

Brief, succinct, well-organized and well-prepared pitches that convey the essence of a story are cited by more than half of these contributors as essential to achieving success. Or more precisely, including lots of unnecessary information and details about characters and plot is repeatedly cited as the primary weakness of most bad pitches.

The other two hallmarks of successful pitches mentioned numerous times are: a great idea — an original, exciting, high-concept story that simply sounds like a great book or movie; and the writer's excitement and passion.

And in case you think I might have stacked the deck and only included responses that support my own ideas, notice that several buyers suggest things that are the opposite of what I recommend (particularly when it comes to the structure of the presentation, and whether the log line, title and genre should begin the pitch).

I'm not including these sometimes contradictory opinions and suggestions to confuse you, but rather to emphasize that there's more than one way to design a successful pitch. Incorporate the ideas that make the most sense to you, and which best suit your own story, style and personality.

In other words, as I've said before, you must make the pitch your own. These added principles and insights will help you do just that.

To get everyone's comments and suggestions, I asked them each the same two questions:

1. *What are the most common weaknesses in the short pitches you've heard, either over the phone or at conferences and pitch fests?*

2. *Think of a specific short pitch — from a writer, agent, manager or executive — that got you to read a screenplay or manuscript. What was it about the pitch that persuaded you?*

Rather than repeat these questions each time, I'll just provide their answers, numbered. (Some respondents combined their thoughts and suggestions into one answer, so those aren't numbered.) Here are their replies:

Jeff Arch
Labrador Media Group
Oscar-nominated Screenwriter: *Sleepless in Seattle*; *Iron Will*; *Saving Millie*
Writer/Director: *Dave Barry's Complete Guide to Guys*; *Two Weeks in Chelsea*

1. The number one weakness I've noticed is that the writer doesn't really have a whole story thought out, yet is able to describe the opening scene in full, Technicolor detail. As soon as I hear the words "*Well, it begins...,*" my radar starts beeping that there's not likely to be a middle or an end. Unfortunately that's true almost 100% of the time.

2. Quite often, if a pitch comes to me from an agent, manager or executive, it also comes with an offer attached, and that tends to be very persuasive. But in other cases, the factors are always the same: There was a clever idea; clear-cut characters; a hero I cared about; a forward motion through a solid story that had a beginning/middle/end; and that elusive "something extra" that made me really want to read the script.

    If the person has those major factors nailed down, that tells me he/she is a professional, and very serious about what they're doing and where they want to go. Because like everyone else, I'm a sucker for a good idea — but more than that, if I'm sitting across from a person who has his/her act together, there's no way I'm going to miss the opportunity to read what they've written.

Adryenn Ashley
21st Century Pictures Group
Producer

1. Lack of originality. Don't tell me it's Cowboys and Indians in Space (*Star Wars*). Don't pitch using references to movies nobody has seen. Keep it fresh, timely, articulate, and interesting.

2. One writer came up with "*The boogieman falls in love with the tooth fairy and has to turn over a new leaf to prove himself.*" I was instantly intrigued. That's what I look for. Keep it simple but interesting, and be able to go into a lot longer but equally as interesting explanation of what happens.

Jenean D. Atwood
Writer, Co-Founder: Atwood Legacy Enterprises

1. People sound terrified! Writers should learn to channel that nervous energy into the pitch. Why should anyone else believe in the project if the pitcher sounds shaky!?

    Do the homework. Know the project, the market and the target audience. Pitchers must be able to answer questions and discuss the project beyond the rehearsed pitch. In an age of multiple platforms, pitchers must be able to show how their content works for other media like cable and wireless.

2. Presentation and preparation are crucial. With these two elements, even the stupid ideas grow legs! With a clear and concise presentation (e.g. *Taxi* meets *Girlfriends*), the person taking the pitch has an automatic reference point. Preparation is a given — the more the better. The pitcher might not use all that has been prepared, but it is better to leave a pitch having not used everything than to wish you had gone the extra mile.

Stanley M. Brooks
Once Upon A Time Films
Producer: *Broken Trail*; *Cool Money*; *Murder at the Presidio*; *Ladies Night*; *On Thin Ice*; *Behind the Mask*; *Beautiful Girl*
Senior Lecturer: The American Film Institute Center for Advanced Film & Television Studies

1. The biggest mistake neophyte writers and producers make is that they focus on the plot (story) and forget to spend the majority of time cementing the concept and the characters. It's the IDEA and the CHARACTERS that get us excited. You can't find those. You can't fix those. You can give notes on plot all day long. That's the least important part of a pitch.

2. The thing that usually sparks my interest is a personal connection to the story from the producer or writer. For example, "*My childhood was spent on a farm and I watched my parents lose it to a big corporation — this story is loosely based on my experiences.*" Passion and emotion sell pitches. If I can sense that in the writer or producer, I'm immediately hooked.

Philippa Burgess
Partner, Creative Convergence

1. One of the greatest weaknesses of most pitches is a lack of understanding of who the writer is pitching to and what that person can or cannot do for them. It is important for a writer to come to the table with endorsements from people who have read and recommended their script, not just that the writer thinks it is saleable to Hollywood. This is a very social business, and information, know-how and contacts have currency.

As a literary manager I've sold a number of pitches to Hollywood and I have heard hundreds upon hundreds of pitches at dozens of conferences around the country. The first thing I like to know is if the person pitching is an amateur or a professional, because we can only hope to make money for professionals. The primary difference is that an amateur wants us to market his script, and a professional wants us to let him know how to make his script marketable. It's a subtle but huge difference.

This is a business, it's not the lottery, and I am interested in someone who takes his craft seriously and is taking practical steps to develop his career. Participation at a screenwriting conference is a step, but it helps if he can mention how long he's been writing, who are his mentors/coaches/teachers, any relevant professional experience (e.g. a law background, if they are writing legal-themed material), what contests have they placed in or won, who they know in the industry, where they are from, and what they are looking to achieve — and all in 30 seconds.

Relationships are key, and I begin to form a relationship with someone the second I lay eyes on them. While I am listening I am trying to assess how far along they are in their path and if they are actually ready for representation. It's easier if they have some "it" factor with a translatable success in another area that we can use to platform them as a screenwriter. I am looking at them considering if I would enjoy working closely with this person, and if I would feel confident introducing them to people in the industry. I also want to know if they are willing to do the work that will be necessary for them to have a sustainable career. Mostly I want to know if they "get it" in terms of knowing and accepting certain "realities" about the business.

Diane Cairns
Producer, Writer, Director; CEO of CAIRNSCO
Productions; Former Senior Vice-President and Head of
West Coast Literary, International Creative
Management; former Senior Vice-President of
Production, Universal Pictures

1. The writer didn't take the time to construct (and rehearse!) a one-line/two-line log line that is brief, accurately descriptive and entertaining.

   A pitch should catch my attention and hold it, promising me/the buyers/the audience a fulfilling movie-going experience. Provoke me to spend time and money to satisfy my piqued curiosity. Don't just tell me the idea — sell me the idea. And don't bother to come to me unless you have a completed screenplay. I am not interested in pitches, treatments or other short-cuts to fame and fortune — ever!!! If you didn't believe in the idea enough to write it, why should I?

   If you call me on the phone, don't babble, don't gush, and don't give me your life story, or even the five-minute version of your pitch. First ask if this is a convenient time to chat, tell me who you are, where you came from and/or how you found me. Then give me the log line of your screenplay. If I'm interested (or more to the point, if I can squeeze in the time), I will tell you then and there. If you have "it," trust that I will know it and respond. Cajoling, campaigning or other hard-selling won't get me to change my mind, and is largely disrespectful.

2. Most of the time, when I agree to read or meet someone, it's not so much that they pitched me something well (because most do it so poorly), but because in their brief solicitation, I am persuaded by whoever recommended them to me, or I'm intrigued by something about their general background, or I take a particular

interest in an arena or a character that I feel will attract another contact's interest.

In other words, if Universal Chairman Ron Meyer recommended you to me, or if you went to USC, or lived in Alaska, or are a twin, or if your idea includes something I think is right for Julia Roberts or Adrian Lyne, you're in. Simply put, you and the log line of your screenplay should, to a large extent, sell themselves on face value.

Deborah Calla
Calla Productions
Producer: *Dream House*; *Lost Zweig*; *Lehi's Wife*;
Fox Kids Club

1. A pitch that is solely based on a one-idea hook. You can tell the writer had one strong idea but didn't put the time into developing it into a story with a beginning, middle and an end. Usually that tells me the writer is inexperienced.

2. An interesting, feasible and well thought-out idea transmitted with enthusiasm will get anyone to read a screenplay or manuscript.

Terra Chalberg
Associate Editor, Simon Spotlight Entertainment/Simon & Schuster

1. Not being specific enough (using words like "event" or "crisis"), and telling too little of the story (as in not reaching the climax, where the character[s] must make a decision of some sort).

2. Pitches that include a thoughtful analysis of the marketplace. Who would buy this book? Why? What successful titles can you compare it to?

Sharon Y. Cobb
Screenwriter: *Lighthouse Hill*; *On Hostile Ground*;
Just Write
Author: *False Confessions of a True Hollywood Screenwriter*

1. As a teacher, I have heard many pitches, and the first script I wrote for real money was based on one of my original pitches. I also sold a movie to Fox 2000, and an MOW that aired on TBS, based on original pitches with partners. Though some of these apply more to pitch meetings than to short pitches, here are a couple of things I've learned over the years:

• You must be "off-paper" when pitching. Meaning you have to memorize the pitch. That being said, I usually took "cue-cards" with me as a safety net during the pitch.

• The pitch must be delivered like you've just thought of it, not like you're repeating lines from a memorized pitch.

• If you can't convey your excitement about the story and characters, no one else will be excited about it.

• Taking acting lessons helps, because to get the producer involved in the emotion of the story is difficult, but if the pitcher gets sincerely emotional about a special moment in the story, the producer may feel the emotion too.

• Introducing characters at the beginning of a pitch and saying a line or two about them is good. But keep it down to three main characters or the producer will get confused.

• Instead of using the characters' names, consider using the role they play in the story, like "*the father.*" That way the producer doesn't have to think, "Wait, who is Oscar?" and then get lost in the pitch.

- There are so many common ideas out there a writer must come up with a unique twist and hyperbolic characters to get a producer's attention.

The biggest mistakes I see:

- Including a bunch of secondary characters I don't care about in the pitch. Start the pitch with an emotional hook into the main character, so I engage with his or her struggles.

- Not enough conflict, inner and outer. The best pitches convey the hard choices the characters must make during their journey through the story.

- An unenthusiastic tone. If the writer isn't excited about the story and characters, I won't be.

- Not enough emotion. If it's a comedy, make me laugh. If it's a drama, make me feel sad or angry or the emotion the character is feeling. If it's a thriller, make my heart race. If it's a slasher movie, make me puke.

When I was teaching at the Santa Fe Screenwriters Conference, one of my students, who was of Native American descent, told me a brief story over lunch one day. The story was fresh, emotional and made me feel the characters were real people, not manufactured entities to carry a story forward.

The pitch broke all the rules. It wasn't high concept. It was quiet and drew me in. I cared about the selfless characters and the heartbreaking choices they had to make. Maybe it was because the story had a setting I'd never heard before. Maybe it was the people and their struggles in the story. Whatever it was, by the end of the pitch, I knew I had to read the script.

Devorah Cutler-Rubenstein
CEO, The Script Broker
Author: *What's the Big Idea? Writing Award Winning Shorts*

1. Calling it a short pitch may throw some folks. What people need to realize is that this first contact is a 'snap shot' photo op — a tease to entice a read from a buyer. Yes, short is good, but it is often not so sweet for most beginners, a little too eager to sell. Often a "pitcher" will throw it out there too fast (too much information overload) or they will race through the story without making a focused connection (what I call a "thoughtless info dump").

    There is an architecture to a great short pitch, just like any great dance, song or piece of art: a beginning (you connect); a middle (you develop the connection by creating a question — born of passion — that interests you both); and an end (there is realistic interest in YOU, if not in your story). Sometimes, nerves backfire and you bore with too many unimportant details.

    You gotta focus. Be clear about the big important beats. Don't tell your story. What is it that you truly want the audience to feel? A great short pitch will make sure the genre is clear. And will make the market/demographics easily apparent. Don't be afraid to show (not tell) you care about your story. If you don't care (too blasé), they can't get excited either.

2. One of the best short pitches I ever heard was from agent-turned-producer/manager, Victoria Wisdom. It was one of those "*Imagine you have only two days to live…*" kind of pitches. Smart. Obvious. But extremely fresh. It started with two questions that were so compelling — so human and universal — that by the end of her two-minute pitch all of us in the room were dying to know how the story turned out.

She put us in the shoes of the protagonists — where we were dragged, bound and gagged along with them. We identified with the dilemma and the big theme, and we were dying to know how WE were going to get out of that impossible situation.

Always, it's that idea where you see the soul behind the concept, and you wish you'd come up with it.

Paul Dinas
Senior Acquisitions Editor, Alpha Books/Penguin USA

1. My pet peeves include: pitches that are inappropriate for my program or list; unclear, rambling descriptions that talk around the project rather than directly to it; no comparisons to similar works already in the marketplace; no direct answer to "Who's the market?"; no clear idea of why this author is the best one for the project.

2. Energy and confidence in the presentation. Humorous insights into the marketplace. Precision — why this is stronger than any other pitch on the topic. Emphasis on the author's expertise or their platform for promotion.

Rona Edwards & Monika Skerbelis
Edwards Skerbelis Entertainment
Producers; Consultants
Authors: *I Liked It, Didn't Love It: Screenplay Development from the Inside Out*

1. The most common weaknesses we encounter are:

    • The writer is not able to articulate the premise in a couple sentences, or reveal the major beats of their story and the main characters in three to five minutes.

    • The writer is unsure of the genre.

    • Some writers compare their story to two films, but

once you hear the pitch it's nothing like the films they are referring to.

- The writer overcomplicates the story with unnecessary information that doesn't move the story forward.

2. We heard a 15-minute family comedy pitch from a young writer who was articulate in pitching the story. We were able to visualize the plotting as it unfolded, and we clearly understood and related to the main character.

The writer also had smart answers to our questions, and we were able to brainstorm on the spot, so we invited the writer to send us the screenplay. After reading the screenplay we had some notes for the writer who handled them with intelligence, and eventually we optioned the material.

Daniel Fridell
Noble Productions, Sweden
Writer/Director: *Cry*; *Swedish Beauty*; *Say That You Love Me*
Producer: *At Point Blank*; *Bloodbrothers*; *Children of Buena Vista*

1. I hear lots of (usually dreadful) short pitches. If they don't catch me in the first sentences, they never do. It has to be edgy, high concept or original, otherwise I have to do the job for them.

Very seldom do I get a pitch where I engage in the character from the beginning, or one with a splendid start scene or sequence that makes me want to know more. I want to be told about something I didn't know about, a story that's exciting and is worth listening to, and is therefore worth telling, or making into a movie.

2. After a while you've heard all the stories; then it's the original subject matter that's important. Someone once

told me that in Kurdistan, criminals use birds as torpe-does and as thieves — they let the birds transport poison into peoples' food and train them to steal other people's birds. Then he started the pitch. That made me read the story, and then invest in the film — an original idea about something I didn't have a clue even existed.

Ginger Earle
Screenwriter; Development Executive: TV/Film Seminars and Workshops; Screenwriting Instructor: California State University Northridge

1. One thing that will immediately reveal that you're an amateur is bringing props or promotional materials, such as photos of stars who could play each major role, business cards or flyers promoting your script. This will also reveal something terrible (but possibly true) about your script: It's been around a long time. It also means your idea isn't fresh and new anymore.

   Of course, in reality you'll rework your scripts for years before even trying to sell them. But buyers don't want to read old, overworked and previously rejected material. So no matter how old, overworked and pre-viously rejected your script actually is, using props in your pitch proves that you've been shopping this idea around for a long time. No one else wanted it, so why would we?

   While working at Miramax, my supervisor told me that he'd actually rather see a script with typos and spelling errors than one with a fancy cover and color pictures, because the typos mean that the story is so hot off the press, so new and fresh and original, that the writer didn't even have time to proof it, let alone come up with headshots of all the potential actors that could star in it.

Julian Friedmann
Literary Agent
Editor: *ScriptWriter Magazine* (London)

1. They are too long; they start in the wrong place; they try to tell you the story rather than what kind of story it is; they fail to give you a connection between the writer and the story and — very common — they are bad ideas for movies and could be stage or radio plays.

2. "*A mother realizes that her teenage son has probably killed someone.*" I was hooked because I knew the way in, that I would get caught up emotionally, and that there would probably be a tough and moving payoff. Actually, the script didn't quite live up to the pitch (another reason not to take pitches too seriously).

Ken Greenblatt
Literary/Talent Agent, Paradigm

1. The most common pitching mistake is not hooking me into the idea quickly. I need to know what the "big concept" is right up front. Also, I'm often surprised when a writer is pitching a comedy and yet fails to make me laugh during the pitch. I need some assurance that the writer knows comedy.

2. When I'm hearing a pitch from a new writer, I'm listening for the new high-concept idea. It must be fresh and original. If I believe that the movie hasn't been done before, is relevant today, and is "highly castable," then I'm in.

Jon Gunn
Lucky Crow Films, IndieProducer.net
Director/Producer/Writer: *My Date with Drew*; *Mercy Streets*

1. The most common weakness is pitches that are unfocused. A good pitch should start general and get more specific. Give me an idea of what kind of movie you're pitching me ("an action adventure set in India") before you tell me funny lines of dialogue or the quirky characteristics of your hero. I recommend the following steps:

   One: Tell the title of the script and genre.

   Two: In a few sentences, explain the plot in broad strokes: "A lonely New York bookkeeper discovers a treasure map in an old almanac, and decides to travel to India to find a priceless historical artifact. On the way, he meets a beautiful young woman who is also searching for the treasure. After falling for her, he realizes she has been sent to kill him once he has decoded the map. But his intelligence and bravery win her over, and together they thwart her evil employers and share the treasure."

   Three: Now fill in the details and anecdotes that make your story unique. Help the person you're pitching to see the movie in their head. Here's where you can help them understand the specific tone of your script. Explain especially fun sequences or memorable moments that will leave them wanting to read the screenplay.

2. Sometimes it's as simple as a great concept with a great title. Other times I've been persuaded by a comparison to a film I love: "It's a British version of *Rushmore*." (Yes, that does sometimes work.) But usually it's something specific and unique.

If I respond well to the concept and then the p[
pitching tells me "stories" about certain scenes tha
funny or powerful, I find that I want to read the v
thing. Most importantly, a great pitch is always confident
and passionate.

Matt Hader
Screenwriter; Producer; Board Member: The American Screenwriter's Association

1. Short pitches should be short — and sweet. The quicker the better. Often times, they're not. If a person can make their point and get the producer to agree to read their screenplay with the fewest words possible, most times it shows they'll also have a succinct storytelling sense.

2. It was a great "what if" type pitch. Especially because the killer "what if" was followed by an even stronger "and then" scenario. Short, sweet and to the point.

Heather Hale
Heather Hale Productions
Writer/Producer: *The Courage to Love*; *The Evidence*; *Lifestyle Magazine*; *Dollar$ and Sense*; *Psychology: The Human Experience*

1. Writers who ramble on and on and on and on, who don't know their own story well enough to share it, who stumble over the details (e.g. too many names for either of us to keep straight), who aren't committed enough to their own choices to defend or clarify them, or who don't reveal the genre until halfway through the pitch — or worse, until they're done.

   In more cases than not, it's the writer's passion. I wonder, "What is it about this story that has gotten so under his/her skin that he/she is compelled to tell it?" That piques my interest.

2. Sometimes it's hearing my own words describing what I was looking delivered back to me effectively. One writer had scoured my former production company's website, and had done his research and due diligence on me, my company and what we were all about. He described his story as "sexy Disney," which was the exact phrase we had used in our own material.

Writers who have won multiple contests with their screenplays, who have genuine interest from professionals in the industry, or who show a pattern of third-party endorsements, will certainly be of interest as well.

Janet Harrison
CEO and Producer, Gothambeach Entertainment

1. Trying to tell too much of the story is probably the most common weakness. It makes the pitch too long, unfocused and, ultimately, usually boring. Instead of being left with wanting to know more and that being the focus of my questions, I end of up asking questions as I try to figure out, "What is the story?"

2. What persuades me is always a combination of passion, the ability of the "pitcher" to quickly create a visual picture for me and a unique story. I have to be left with the feeling of "wanting to know more."

Alli Hartley
Director of Development, Tomorrow Films

1. I hate it when people tell me how to sell a script, especially if they're new writers. You don't need to tell me a script has a strong female lead, or will be marketable because of its similarity to whatever blockbuster. It's my job to know that. It also wastes time that you should be spending on telling your story.

I also hate it when writers or managers bring in a personal anecdote to explain how powerful their story is. If you care about your drug addict heroine because a friend struggled with drug addiction, it's sad, but it doesn't tell me whether or not you're a good writer. In these cases, I just end up feeling like the author is trying to manipulate me into reading the script out of pity.

2. If the author can deliver a joke well, that's huge. A joke is a story unto itself, and if the author's joke is well timed, set up and delivered, it says to me something about his knowledge of the mechanics of storytelling. It also says something about his sense of humor and personal writing style.

John E. Johnson
Avon Fields Productions
Executive Director, American Screenwriters Association

1. The most common weakness in short pitches I've heard is that the pitch is not told succinctly, passionately and in a manner that would entice me to want to know more. Writers need to remember they aren't pitching "a script" — the words on the page — they're pitching the whole movie. What's the point of your story, and why is it worth telling? Who are the main characters, why should we care about them and what's at stake for them if they don't succeed?

2. The pitch left the person's mouth, entered my psyche and wouldn't let go until I begged to know more.

Simon Kinberg
Genre Films, Inc.
Screenwriter, Producer: *Mr. and Mrs. Smith*; *X-Men 3*

1. I think the biggest weakness is always about scope. Often, writers and producers don't realize that pitches are not screenplays or movies. They're a separate medium, with separate narrative conventions. You can't tell the entire film in 15 to 20 minutes. You need to aggressively condense the story and characters. You need to sell the big idea, then use the basic story structure and character arcs to underpin that idea. It's like a trailer for a movie — you are only selling the most salient points.

    I think good pitches are structured like newspaper articles. You have the big headline — the hook. Then the first paragraph gives you the overall story and main characters. Then the body of the article gets into the details. In my experience, good pitches tend to spend a lot of time on the first act (setup) and third act (payoff), without dwelling on all the machinations of the second act.

2. It was the basic idea — fresh and original, but also conforming to existing genres. It's a difficult balance — because audiences want new voices, new stories, but they also want the familiar package when it comes to commercial films. I know that any pitch I've sold as a writer always looks a bit like another successful movie (for instance, *Mr. and Mrs. Smith* resembling *True Lies*), but they're fundamentally different under the surface.

Ken Lee
Vice President, Michael Wiese Productions

1. A short pitch should have four things: a brilliant introduction of the person who is pitching that establishes
   their credibility; a strong hook for the subject matter that
   establishes the unique qualities of the project; a clear
   understanding of the target market; and a realistic
   assessment of the market potential.

2. I like it when a pitch blends the abstract part of the business with the analytical part of the business effortlessly.

Ken Levine
Writer/Producer: *M*A*S*H; *Cheers*; *Frasier*; *The
Simpsons***

1. They start pitching the story before telling me the log
   line. When they're talking and I'm thinking, "What is
   this about?" they're dead.

2. A great idea. A "*Damn! Wish I had thought of that!*" idea.

Paul S. Levine
Entertainment Attorney, Literary Agent

1. People assuming I know what they're talking about.
   They tell me a story from the middle to the end, and
   forget to tell me the beginning, so I have no idea what
   they're talking about.

2. It was a pitch from a former journalist. In my experience, journalists are the best people at telling a story in
   terms of who, what, where, why, when and how. And
   they cover all of that in the very first paragraph of their
   pitch. So a pitch that tells me where we are, when we
   are, who we're talking about, what happens, etc — the
   basic elements of the story.

Frederick Levy
Management 101
Producer: *Unknown*; *Frailty*

1. The biggest mistake people make is they're just not pre-
    pared. They sign up for these pitch fests a month or
    two in advance, they know it's coming, they know
    they've got five minutes or ten minutes or whatever the
    time constraint is, and they know what they need to be
    able to convey in that short amount of time, yet they
    do very little preparation to actually be able to make a
    sensible pitch.

    I feel like 90% of the people I meet at these festivals
    didn't put any thought into what they were going to say
    to me. They just show up and say, "Let me tell you about
    the story I wrote." Which would be okay if they were
    able to tell me about the story they wrote, but most of
    them get too nervous and flub it up.

    You need to be prepared at all times. You have no idea
    when the opportunity will come — you're at a cocktail
    party and somebody says, "Oh, what are you working on?"
    Boom — you go into your pitch. If you're not prepared,
    how are you going to seize those opportunities?

2. I'm not sure if I can pinpoint a specific one, because I've
    heard so many, but I can say this: *the more high concept your
    idea, the easier it is to pitch*. You can pitch a high-concept
    idea in one sentence and get me hooked and excited.

    Pitching a drama is the most difficult task there is,
    because dramatic or epic or period movies can't be
    summed up in a line. It takes ten or twenty minutes to
    develop the characters and the story so the other person
    understands what you're getting at. Pitching a comedy or
    genre film is much more doable. Pitching is a very
    important skill, but I think it's more appropriate for some
    stories than for others.

Christopher Lockhart
Executive Story Editor, ICM

1. A common weakness is the failure to communicate the heart of the story — the core of the drama. In a short pitch, there isn't a lot of time to dwell on the unnecessary. The writer must get to the most important piece of information: what the story is about. There's lots of talk about backstory and setup, but the writer fails to let us see the dramatic throughline of the screenplay, which is often communicated through the log line.

    However, the biggest weakness may be that writers fail to allow the listener to "see the movie." A good pitch should enable me to see the movie, picture the stars, understand the demographics, know how many screens it will open up on, and even envision the poster. "*A New York City cop travels to Los Angeles to reconcile with his wife but learns she's been taken hostage by terrorists in a sky-scraper — and he struggles alone to save her. It's called* Die Hard." In a nutshell, that allows us see the dramatic throughline, the trajectory of the story and helps us envision the other factors that go into selling movies.

    Writers should never discount the importance of a title in a pitch either. A good title can be half the battle. The often-mocked title *Snakes on a Plane* told the whole story and got the writers their payday.

2. It was the concept. It's almost always about the concept. Short pitches benefit from a concise concept — one that creates lots of conflict. What's most important is that I get a sense that what I'm hearing can sustain a 120-page script. After all, I have to invest two hours to read it.

    I have heard good pitches that are character driven and don't offer much of a concept — but the protagonist is unique and compelling and seems like he could carry the weight of the story. Pitches that work intrigue me, move me and make me want to see the movie.

Bill Lundy
Screenwriter, Script Consultant

1. Not saying what the genre is up front, not giving the title of the script, not saying who (or what) the protagonist and antagonist are, focusing on unimportant details or subplots instead of the primary story arc, ignoring the emotional journey of the protagonist and not wanting to give a hint of how the story ends.

2. An incredibly brilliant concept. In this case, a sci-fi take on a piece of classic literature. Something I wish I'd thought of myself and can't wait to see on the screen.

Suzanne Lyons
Snowfall Films and WindChill Films
Producer: *Undertaking Betty*; *Jericho Mansions*; *Bailey's Billon\$*; *The Heart Is Deceitful Above All Things*; *Candy Stripers*
Co-founder, Flash Forward Institute

1. People (writers are the worst) are too vague, too wordy and too flowery; they use too many adjectives that don't tell me anything. We just want to know what the story is about! I also hate hearing, "This is my life story." It makes me crazy.

2. When the pitch is really clear. Right away, I know what the genre is and what format it is in (script, treatment, etc). As the pitch continues I am clear who the protagonist is, and about the theme, the beginning, the middle and the end. Just these simple things make all the difference for me to make my decision as to whether or not it is something for my company.

    It also helps when there is enthusiasm, when the

words they choose reflect the tone of the project, and when they tell me what's new, what's exciting, what's the hook! Why is it a movie and not an MOW? If a studio is going to put $15 million into making it, and you've got three killer sentences (60 seconds) to get us hooked, each sentence better be worth $5 million!!!

Paul Margolis
Screenwriter: *John Carpenter's The 13th Apostle*; *Ticker*
Writer/Producer: *Pacific Blue*; *Sirens*; *MacGyver*
Professor of Film: Brooks Institute

1. I guess I've been fortunate in that I've sold pitches to almost every studio, and a whole bunch of TV shows as well. So on some level, I feel like I've made pitching work for me in my career, in spite of the fact that I hate doing it. And certainly I've heard a lot of pitches; not only as a teacher, but also on the different TV shows I've worked on and produced. I've heard tons of writers come in to pitch stories, as well as agents pitching a particular client who had an idea for an episode. And what it all really comes down to is the concept.

    It really doesn't matter how skillful you are as a pitcher. There are people who are better than others, there's no doubt about that. But when I think about the pitches that I've sold, and the ones that I've bought as a producer on TV shows, it's always just been about a great premise. So my hugest piece of advice would be, if you don't have an incredibly great concept, it doesn't matter how good your pitches are.

    I've had stories that I thought were good, but they weren't great, and I've gone all over town trying to pitch them to big producers, and they haven't been bought. And then I'd have other situations where I didn't feel confident about the pitch I was doing, but the idea was fantastic, and it got bought.

People want to spend all this time and energy trying to figure out how to become master salesmen, and their energy is in the wrong place. They should put all that hard work — that seat-of-the-pants work — into figuring out, "Where is the greatness in the idea that I'm trying to develop?"

If I tell you an idea, and I have to ask you what did you think about it, then I should throw it in the trash. It's not good enough. I tell you as a person that's sold scripts and written stories, there's a certain sort of passion that you have about a story when you know it's right. You don't have to ask anybody — you can feel it in your blood.

I once heard a producer say something to me that has always stuck in my head, and it was brilliant as far as I'm concerned. He said, "I have had more writers come in here and pitch and sell me a story in the first five minutes, and then unsell it in the next five minutes." In other words, you can go too long on a pitch. You see that look in their eye like they're into it, and you feel the necessity to keep going, and to tell more, instead of just shutting up, and walking away with a check.

Kate McCallum
Bridge Arts Media
Founder: Center for Conscious Creativity

1. A writer will ramble on and not get to the point or describe the genre up front. Or they start right in telling a story that is not succinct. Better to start with "*This is a drama about…*" or "*This is a romantic comedy.*" When you do this it automatically gets a listener engaged in a style, a tone, etc. I also like a one-liner up front, which can follow the genre description.

2. Material based on true stories, books, etc., is always something that piques my interest. Or if the writer has

specific expertise in the area the story is set in, or the type of character they've created. I am always interested in stories that push boundaries as well — stories that are innovative or unique.

Esther Newberg
Senior Vice President, Co-Director, Literary
Department, International Creative Management

The worst pitch I ever heard was at an ICM meeting with literary agents 25 years ago or more. It was from a television guy who said he was looking for *Jaws*, but with a tiger. The agent who repped Tennessee Williams got up and left the room.

Signe Olynyk
Writer/Producer
Creator of the Great American PitchFest

Pitching is a necessary evil, and it doesn't come naturally to everyone. The good news is that for most writers, it usually gets better with practice. That's where pitch fests and conferences are so important. They allow you the opportunity for critical "face time" with agents and production companies. At the Great American Pitch Fest, most participants meet with an average of 20 companies — which means they get to practice a lot of pitches.

Producer Suzanne Lyons, who also runs the Flash Forward Institute, once estimated she had to give an average of 200 pitches before she sold a project. She has a great approach to pitching: every time she gives one that doesn't sell, she looks at it as, "*That's one more pitch closer to a sale.*" She's right. You can't sell your project if you don't pitch it.

The best pitches are:

- Sincere – the person pitching *loves* these characters and really cares about the story. They get excited talking about it. To say they are "passionate" sounds corny, but it's true. This story is bursting out of them, and it engages the listener.

- Populated with *relatable* characters that are interesting and unique. Stereotypical characters are flat because they're predictable and stale. I want to be intrigued by characters I can identify with, but who do and say things that haven't been said or done before. Fresh is the key.

- Clear & Concise. The first thing I want to know is the genre (thriller, comedy, etc.) if it is a movie script, or format (series, sitcom, etc.) if it's for TV. Then I want to know who the protagonist is, what they want, what their key obstacles are, and what they must do to overcome those obstacles — all in one or two tight sentences. Then I want to know the most important thing: What has the protagonist discovered about themselves by the end of the script? If the "lesson learned" is a universal theme or truth that interest me, and the rest of the pitch suggests a well structured screenplay, I will request the script.

- Unpredictable. They pose questions that haven't been asked before. A great pitch always leaves me wanting more.

The worst pitches:

- ...do not have a log line, the protagonist's goal is unclear, and the writer insists on telling me every detail of their script from beginning to end. If a writer has not invested the time to learn how to pitch or develop a log line, it is unlikely they have mastered their craft as a writer. I hear and read hundreds of pitches every year. I want to work with professionals. A professional screenwriter knows how to pitch *and* how to write. They are skills that are equally important.

- …are from people who pretend to be knowledgeable about my company, and our credits. Please don't lie to me and say you loved our films if you've never seen them. Whenever possible, try to research a company and know as much about them as you can. With the resources available, such as the Internet and trade papers, there is never an excuse for not knowing about a company. However, you can't know everything. It's reasonable to ask questions if you don't know things about a company. Just don't lie. There's enough of that already in this business.

- …focus on selling the script versus building a relationship. As a producer and a creative person, I want to work with people I like and connect with. Chemistry is just as important to me as the story being pitched. In every meeting, I am evaluating whether the writer is someone I can spend the next six months, or longer, working closely with. Are they responsive to my questions and comments? Do they seem pleasant and easy to work with? Selling a script is not just about selling the script — it is also about selling yourself.

- …are when the writer has nothing else to pitch. Always have at least two more well polished pitches ready, just in case. If none of your pitches is right for that individual, use any remaining time to find out more information. What are they looking for? For film, or TV? What budgets? Is there a particular star or director they want to work with? Go on an "information quest" and use your time as effectively as possible, either to learn more, or to develop your relationship with them further. Every pitch meeting is an opportunity — to pitch yourself, AND to pitch your scripts. Whether it's a phone call, an email, a pitch fest meeting, or a query letter, it is a chance to build a relationship with someone who can help build your screenwriting career.

Neil Pennella
President, Enora Productions
Television and Internet Content Producer

1. Clearly, the most aggravating aspect of a weak pitch is the inability to articulate the concept within a minute or less. It ranks up there in frustration with a lack of knowledge about the subject matter. I don't mind if the idea is a bit fuzzy, as long as the communicator is enthusiastic and is willing to go into greater detail once you begin to question him/her.

   As with all discourse, particularly presenting a new concept, shorter and less complex sentence structures are always appreciated. And I do not appreciate a presenter taking up any real time explaining why a competitor's idea was not good.

2. I think back to a manuscript recently submitted about which the producer got me excited over the content of the piece. The pitch both challenged me and at the same time intrigued me. He asked me a provocative question: "What if I could explain to you that Shakespeare was not the author of any of 'his' plays? How exciting would it be to find out who really wrote the plays of Shakespeare?" It got my attention to think that this literary giant was only the 'front man' for far

more urbane and intellectual persons who, for their own good reasons, did not want to be identified with playwriting. I just had to know more: it was the provocative question about subject matter that was important to me, an English Literature major in college, which wholly captured my attention.

Jim Pasternak
FilmDaDa
Directing Teacher, Producer, Director: *Certifiably Jonathan*

For me the ideal pitch is a short sentence that makes me laugh or gasp. The idea/premise/log line pitched is such an incongruous surprise that I have an involuntary response. Nothing intellectual can surpass or negate that initial reaction.

Terry Rossio
Screenwriter (with Ted Elliott): *Aladdin*; *The Mask of Zorro*; *The Road to El Dorado*; *Shrek*; *Pirates of the Caribbean 1, 2,* **and** *3*; **(with Bill Marsilii):** *Deja Vu*

1. Commercial, filmic concepts are hard to come by; most short pitches fail not in presentation, but lack of content. The idea either can't be a movie, or would be very difficult to become a movie, or just shouldn't be a movie.

2. Gold is to hear a story idea on a topic everyone knows, but there's not been a film to exploit it yet. The approach sets up a clear filmic situation, with a promise of a compelling central character relationship. There's a huge difference between "*A student named James studies Korean to overcome feelings of low self-esteem*" and "*A young Shakespeare falls in love as he desperately tries to write and stage* Romeo and Juliet."

Ellen Sandler
Script Consultant, Screenwriter, Co-Executive
Producer: *Everybody Loves Raymond*

1. The most common mistake I hear? Way too many details
    — especially details involving the backstory and setup —
    and not enough consequences, or what I call the *"so
    what?"* factor. A writer will tell me what happens in great
    detail, but there won't be much follow-up as to how that
    changes the character and what the character must do as
    a consequence. I'll hear details, sometimes even camera
    shots, but I won't hear a story.

2. I was doing a demonstration workshop on pitching where
    a participating writer tried to pitch a long, involved caper
    movie which was coming across as complicated, confus-
    ing and going nowhere. I asked her some probing ques-
    tions, and we figured out what it was really about. She
    then came up with one of the best short pitches I ever
    heard: *"It's about two people who are such good friends they're
    willing to kill for each other."*

    I got an immediate identification with the characters,
    I knew they had passion, I knew things would go horri-
    bly wrong for them, I could guess that one or both of
    them would get killed, and most important, I wanted to
    find out how.

    Once you've got a pitch line that good, make sure the
    story matches it. The pitch will only get the script open;
    it's the writing that will keep the pages turning until
    FADE OUT.

Dr. Linda Seger
Script Consultant, Seminar Leader
Author: *Making a Good Script Great*; *Creating Unforgettable Characters*; *Making a Good Writer Great*; *Advanced Screenwriting*

1. Most pitches are too long and don't contain a sense of conflict, or story or character or theme. Writers tend to go on and on, "... and then they did this, and then they did that," so it's a series of episodes, rather than hooking the listener to want the details.

   I usually recommend that people work up an elevator pitch of about 20-60 seconds, and then a pitch of 3-5 minutes, and then a pitch of 15-20 minutes, with all the basic story beats of Act I, II and III. If they can possibly shade in a sense of the conflict, story, character and theme, at least with the longer pitches, that's good too, although sometimes they can shade in some sense of these other elements even in a short pitch.

2. The pitch had conflict and originality. It was a subject matter that I didn't know much about, but that intrigued me. I sensed the person knew what s/he was talking about. I sensed the person had done some study and knew something about screenplays, so that it would be worth my time to read the script. (Of course, I read for a fee, but some pitches make me look forward to the assignment more than others.)

Paul Jay Shrater
Cornucopia Pictures
Writer-Producer

Here are what I consider to be the primary weaknesses of most query letters and pitches, along with rules for improving them:

1. Lack of confidence in presenting your own material. If you aren't enthusiastic about it, why should I be?

2. Overselling. I don't care about some big producer who supposedly loves your work — if he didn't work with you on selling it, there must be a reason why. And I don't need a cover letter full of adjectives about how great the script it.

3. Lack of focused attention. I don't want to see an email that is copied to 100 other producers — it's not worth my time competing for a script when I don't even know if it's good yet.

4. Rambling. If you can't tell me your story in a clear and concise manner, odds are, it's also going to be all over the place on the page.

5. All I need is a hook. Many times, one sentence is all that is needed to get my interest in something. A writer I worked with once called this the *Air Force One* rule, meaning that movie can be pitched as, "Air Force One gets hijacked." That's all you need. In most cases, the hook is what eventually sells the project.

6. Measured follow-ups. Pestering is bad, but follow-up is great. Producers' and executives' schedules are very busy, but if you are on their minds here and there, a small emotional connection can be made. If the follow-up is too often, it can be a nuisance.

7. Don't do the hard sell. Executives and producers evaluate the writer based on whether they would feel comfortable working with them for years. If the writer is difficult from the get-go in regards to deal points and/or collaborative creative issues, even if the script is good, sometimes it will elicit a pass from the executive

or producer. Your time to get the big money is when it actually sells to a studio.

8. Socialize. Sometimes it is best to get to know a person before getting straight to business. If an executive or producer likes you before hearing you pitch them cold, odds are they will look at your stuff — even if its a simple exchange of a few sentences that develops some common ground.

9. Recognize when to pitch and when to wait. Don't be so excited that you are standing next to someone you want to pitch to that you launch right into your pitch. It might be better just to socialize or ask a question. Then, a couple of days later, follow up with a call or a letter including your pitch.

10. There are no set rules of how things get done. You will find advice about what to do and what not to do, but there are numerous ways that things can work. Vary your strategy and find what works best for you.

If someone follows the rules that I outlined above, then I'll generally take a look — assuming the "hook" is something that excites me, and makes me think the property has a chance in the marketplace.

Pamela Jaye Smith
Writer, Consultant, Award-winning Producer-Director
Author: *Inner Drives: How to Write and Create Characters Using the Eight Classic Centers of Motivation*
Founder: Mythworks

1. Too much time setting up the story and/or the main character. Too much about why the person wrote the story (me, me, me). Too much about how much I'm going to like the story, or why it is so commercial.

Basically, too much information that is not specifically about the story itself.

2. Three different approaches I like come to mind:

- **A provocative conflict.** Pairs of opposites (man vs. woman, white vs. black, hobbit vs. wizard, fisherman vs. storm, rebel vs. establishment, etc.) in precarious situations (during the plague, in an election, a war zone, a depression, a space flight, etc.)

- **Identification plus alienation.** An every-person characteristic (rejected lover, grieving widower, ambitious high school grad, talented slacker, commitment-phobe, etc.) confronting the terrifying prospect of change (opening to emotion, taking responsibility, sacrificing for others, risking rejection, etc.)

- **An intriguing, engaging personal question.** "Have you ever wondered what would happen if...?" "You know how sometimes you think, 'If only I could go back in time to...'?" or, "What if your deepest wish came true?" "What's your favorite myth? What if you got to live it?"

Rob Tobin
Award-Winning Screenwriter, Script Consultant, Script Doctor
Author: *How to Write High Structure, High Concept Movies*; and *Screenwriting: The Secret Formula*

As a former development exec, and as someone who is invited to sit as a panelist at pitch fests, the most common weaknesses in the pitches I've heard have to do with the writer not really knowing his or her story well enough to convey it clearly and succinctly. More specifically, the writers don't know the essential elements, and how to incorporate them into a pitchable log line. "*A calloused radio psychologist starts experiencing the neuroses of his call-in patients.*" Though this script has yet to be produced, it sold to a studio the first day it went out to the town. I read it because the pitch had built-in conflict, I knew who the hero was, what the end-of-act-one event was, there was an implied second act, the hero's flaw was in the log line, and all of that in a very short, easily spoken and easily remembered sentence.

Dave Trottier
Author: *The Screenwriter's Bible*; *Dr. Format Answers Your Questions*

1. First, the failure to focus on the character and story. Second, a pitch that is too general. Example of both weaknesses: "*My story is about a Mafia family in turmoil and transition.*" Better: "*When a powerful Mafia don is shot, his reluctant son takes actions that elevate him to become the next godfather.*" A third weakness is trying to force too many subplots into the pitch, rather than focusing on the core story.

2. I don't have permission to share the pitch, but my reaction was, "*Now that's a movie!*" In other words, the pitch presented a clear, focused and unencumbered story concept that naturally translated to the silver screen.

Irena Tully
Managing Director, Impulse Productions

1. Lack of contagious passion about one's own script, and an inability to convey its clear message and magic. Writers' visions are often diminished by rambling about

commercial prospects, or making statements like, "It's going to be one of the best films ever made."

2. This pitch has worked for me: "I *have worked on this story since I was born — I felt through it, lived through it, dreamed through it, laughed and cried through it, and now I'd like others to share my journey. It's about a…*"

I always appreciate a polite yet confident approach, while striking an emotional cord without being familiar. If the pitch comes from an agent or executive, the fact that A-list talent is interested/attached to the project helps in deciding to read it. You want to find out what the others have seen in it and compare that with your own perception.

Mark R. Turner
Above the Line Media
Producer; Board Member: The American Screenwriters Association

1. A common mistake occurs when people try to sound too much like other, existing productions. Simply saying, "*It's like Old Movie A meets Old Movie B in outer space,*" pretty much means you couldn't think of an original way to pitch your story. Use those points of reference, but don't rely on them to be your entire pitch. Otherwise you're telling me that you've basically just re-written a picture or combined two other pictures into something you think is new.

Another common problem is mistaking passion for a good story. Just because it happened to you doesn't make it interesting. Just because you feel passionately about it doesn't mean that it's going to put butts in the seats. It is important to believe in what you are writing and pitching, but always keep in mind that producers and distributors are going to need to sell it to the general public. So tell them what the selling points are. Help them to see why the movie-going public is going to embrace your screenplay as a picture they want to see.

2. Sometimes a great title will generate enough interest for me to want to read the screenplay. At Austin a couple of years back, a writer gave a quick sentence that summed up the story and then told the title. I started laughing, and I knew, even before she went any further, that I wanted to read that screenplay. She used that quick overview as the setup, and the title as if it were the punch line to a joke.

Rodney Vance
Screenwriter: *Conspiracy Café*; *Operation Babylift*; *Under Cover of Darkness*; *Raven Chase*
Head Writer: *The Evidence*; *Lifestyle Magazine*

1. When I ask screenwriters what their script is about, they often launch into a (potentially) lengthy listing of events which are too detailed to keep in my head. If I have time, I ask questions. *"Who's your story about? What is the one thing he/she must achieve in this story? Does he* achieve it? Everything else is detail that quickly becomes confusing.

2. A screenplay pitch I really liked was, *"(Title) is a quirky comedy about a mortician who is kidnapped by a conspiracy of beautiful women, falls in love and saves the world from a nanovirus intended to make men nice."* I liked the pitch because it was funny, told me the essence of the story, and sparked my curiosity about the details. That curiosity made me want to read the script.

Michael Wiese
Michael Wiese Productions
Publisher, Filmmaker

1. The weakness most pitches have is that they don't connect the concept to the market. Regardless of the length of the pitch, the listener should — almost immediately — be able to ascertain the budget level, the marketing elements (cast, genre, hooks) and the market potential.

   When I was an executive at Vestron I bought over 200 videos and heard 3000 pitches a year. The worst pitch I heard was an oldie 60's music compilation that the pitcher played as he "acted out" every shot. When he did "*Splish Splash, I was takin' a bath...*" it was time to end the meeting.

   I was pitched a video in an elevator in NYC once and bought it. But pitching at urinals or slipping scripts under bathroom stalls is unacceptable. Instant pass.

2. Either the project "made some kind of difference" in the world — it would have a powerful effect and change lives — or it was commercial. Or once in a while, both.

   If pitchers were buyers, they'd know how to construct a pitch. Writers know their own needs: Sell the script, the book, the movie. But they need to know the buyer's needs and address those in the pitch. That's why the buyer is listening.

   I remember pitching Don King on a boxing video series. I got the art department to mock up a video box that had Don King's picture on it under the title *Don King Presents Boxing's Greatest Hits*. His picture was much bigger than Ali's or Foreman's. In the meeting I had an assistant count the number of times that King glanced at the box (15 times in one minute!). We met the needs of the person we were pitching!

13

Here's what I consider just about the strongest pitch you can possibly make: *"Hi, my name is James Cameron, and I have a new screenplay."*

Of course, you can't make that pitch, because you're not James Cameron. But you can be, if you write enough good screenplays, and enough of them get produced, and enough of those make a lot of money. Even James Cameron had to convince people to read his stuff once upon a time.

So what's my point?

My point is that the best pitch you'll ever give is the one that results in a deal. *And that will only happen when you can back up your pitch with a great screenplay or a great novel.*

Getting your writing read is terrific. It's the only way to advance your career, and the only way you'll ever achieve money, success, acclaim or fulfillment as a writer. But it's only a step towards those goals. The real obstacle, the real work, and the real reward come with the completion of a novel or screenplay that people want to buy.

Getting anybody at all to read our work can sometimes be so difficult and discouraging that it becomes our sole focus. But even persuading a hundred people to look at your screenplay or book proposal isn't worth a hoot in hell if they all pass.

This is not to say that pitching skills aren't important. Buyers are so jaded by the countless crappy scripts and manuscripts they've had to read that simply getting them to consider you is a challenge. And I don't want your voice to be silenced just because you can't penetrate the filtering system created by the film and book industries. That's why I wrote this book.

But the truth is, a weak pitch of a great story is far more viable than a great pitch of a mediocre one. Because even if you stumble and mumble and go on too long and say all the wrong things, some buyers will see beneath the weaknesses of your pitch to the potential of your story. And they'll agree to read it.

And if they read it, and it's terrific, they'll like it; and if they like it they'll recommend it; and if they recommend it to enough other people who read it and like it, you'll have yourself a deal, in spite of the fact that your pitch was less than dazzling.

This certainly isn't something I would have said in the introduction to this book. I mean, get real — I want this book to sell, and saying up front that a great pitch isn't the most important asset a writer can have could have cost me a bundle in lost royalties. Plus I truly believe that developing your ability to pitch will accelerate your career and make it much easier for you to succeed.

But deep down we both know that the one essential commodity you must have, that you must always have, is a great story. So focus on that; strive for that; master that. Everything else is secondary.

As writers, it's hard for us to accept the fact that great writing rises to the surface. It's much more comforting, and a much better excuse for failure, if we can blame it on readers and agents and producers and executives who can't be approached, and a system that's designed to exclude us. This belief may not make us happy, but it keeps us safe. As long as we're convinced that success is impossible, and that everyone's out to stop us, we can avoid taking any risk.

I'm not denying the difficulty of a writing or filmmaking career, or the obstacles that must be overcome. But I am saying that if hundreds of novels and plays and movies and TV shows are published and produced every year, it's not impossible.

If you're absolutely committed to working every day, and to perfecting your craft, and to putting yourself out there in whatever way is necessary to get your material read — no matter how terrifying that is — then success, and fulfillment, and a chance to be heard and to touch people's lives, will truly be yours.

INDEX

THE WRITER'S JOURNEY
2ND EDITION
MYTHIC STRUCTURE FOR WRITERS

CHRISTOPHER VOGLER

BEST SELLER
OVER 116,500 UNITS SOLD!

See why this book has become an international bestseller and a true classic. *The Writer's Journey* explores the powerful relationship between mythology and storytelling in a clear, concise style that's made it required reading for movie executives, screenwriters, playwrights, scholars, and fans of pop culture all over the world.

Both fiction and nonfiction writers will discover a set of useful myth-inspired storytelling paradigms (i.e., "The Hero's Journey") and step-by-step guidelines to plot and character development. Based on the work of Joseph Campbell, *The Writer's Journey* is a must for all writers interested in further developing their craft.

The updated and revised second edition provides new insights and observations from Vogler's ongoing work on mythology's influence on stories, movies, and man himself.

"This book is like having the smartest person in the story meeting come home with you and whisper what to do in your ear as you write a screenplay. Insight for insight, step for step, Chris Vogler takes us through the process of connecting theme to story and making a script come alive."

> *— Lynda Obst, Producer*
> Sleepless in Seattle, How to Lose a Guy in 10 Days
> *Author*, Hello, He Lied

"This is a book about the stories we write, and perhaps more importantly, the stories we live. It is the most influential work I have yet encountered on the art, nature, and the very purpose of storytelling."

> *— Bruce Joel Rubin, Screenwriter*
> Stuart Little 2, Deep Impact, Ghost, Jacob's Ladder

CHRISTOPHER VOGLER, a top Hollywood story consultant and development executive, has worked on such high-grossing feature films as *The Lion King, The Thin Red Line, Fight Club,* and *Beauty and the Beast.* He conducts writing workshops around the globe.

$24.95 | 325 PAGES | ORDER # 98RLS | ISBN: 0-941188-70-1

SAVE THE CAT!
THE LAST BOOK ON SCREENWRITING YOU'LL EVER NEED

BLAKE SNYDER

BLAKE SNYDER

He's made millions of dollars selling screenplays to Hollywood and now screenwriter Blake Snyder tells all. "Save the Cat" is just one of Snyder's many ironclad rules for making your ideas more marketable and your script more satisfying — and saleable, including:

- The four elements of every winning logline.
- The seven immutable laws of screenplay physics.
- The 10 genres and why they're important to your movie.
- Why your Hero must serve your Idea.
- Mastering the Beats.
- Mastering the Board to create the Perfect Beast.
- How to get back on track with ironclad and proven rules for script repair.

This ultimate insider's guide reveals the secrets that none dare admit, told by a show biz veteran who's proven that you can sell your script if you can save the cat.

"Imagine what would happen in a town where more writers approached screenwriting the way Blake suggests? My weekend read would dramatically improve, both in sellable/producible content and in discovering new writers who understand the craft of storytelling and can be hired on assignment for ideas we already have in house."
> — *From the Foreword by Sheila Hanahan Taylor, Vice President, Development at Zide/Perry Entertainment, whose films include* American Pie, Cats and Dogs *and* Final Destination

"Want to know how to be a successful writer in Hollywood? The answers are here. Blake Snyder has written an insider's book that's informative — and funny, too."
> — *David Hoberman, Producer,* Raising Helen, Walking Tall, Bringing Down the House

"Blake Snyder's Save the Cat! *could also be called* Save the Screenwriter!, *because that's exactly what it will do:* Save the Screenwriter *time,* Save the Screenwriter *frustration, and* Save the Screenwriter's *sanity... by demystifying the Hollywood process."*
> — *Andy Cohen, Literary Manager/Producer; President, Grade A Entertainment*

BLAKE SNYDER has sold dozens of scripts, including co-writing the Disney hit, *Blank Check*, and *Nuclear Family* for Steven Spielberg — both million-dollar sales.

$19.95 | 216 PAGES | ORDER # 34RLS | ISBN: 1-932907-00-9

THE HOLLYWOOD STANDARD
THE COMPLETE AND AUTHORITATIVE GUIDE TO SCRIPT FORMAT AND STYLE

CHRISTOPHER RILEY

Finally, there's a script format guide that is accurate, complete, and easy to use, written by Hollywood's foremost authority on industry standard script formats. Riley's guide is filled with clear, concise, complete instructions and hundreds of examples to take the guesswork out of a multitude of formatting questions that perplex screenwriters, waste their time, and steal their confidence. You'll learn how to get into and out of a POV shot, how to set up a telephone intercut, what to capitalize and why, how to control pacing with format, and more.

"The Hollywood Standard *is not only indispensable, it's practical, readable, and fun to use."*
— *Dean Batali, Writer-Producer,* That '70s Show; *Writer,* Buffy the Vampire Slayer

"*Buy this book before you write another word! It's required reading for any screenwriter who wants to be taken seriously by Hollywood."*
— *Elizabeth Stephen, President, Mandalay Television Pictures;*
Executive Vice President Motion Picture Production, Mandalay Pictures

"*Riley has succeeded in an extremely difficult task: He has produced a guide to screenplay formatting which is both entertaining to read and exceptionally thorough. Riley's clear style, authoritative voice, and well-written examples make this book far more enjoyable than any formatting guide has a right to be. This is the best guide to script formatting ever, and it is an indispensable tool for every writer working in Hollywood."*
— *Wout Thielemans,* Screentalk Magazine

"*It doesn't matter how great your screenplay is if it looks all wrong. The Hollywood Standard is probably the most critical book any screenwriter who is serious about being taken seriously can own. For any writer who truly understands the power of making a good first impression, this comprehensive guide to format and style is priceless."*
— *Marie Jones,* www.absolutewrite.com

CHRISTOPHER RILEY, based in Los Angeles, developed Warner Brothers Studios script software and serves as the ultimate arbiter of script format for the entertainment industry.

$18.95 | 208 PAGES | ORDER # 31RLS | ISBN: 1-932907-01-7

FROM THE AUTHOR

I would love to hear from you about your experience with this book, and with using the principles I've outlined to pitch your novel or screenplay. And if you have any questions about the process, please send them to me through my website below. I can't promise I'll be able to reply to every email, but I regularly post my answers to questions about writing and pitching on my website. And please know that your taking the time to connect with me is deeply appreciated.

And of course, if you would ever like help and coaching in designing and perfecting your pitch, or in creating and writing your story, screenplay, or novel, please contact me through my website at *www.ScreenplayMastery.com*.

Now good luck with your pitch, keep writing, and stay with your passion!

MICHAEL HAUGE

2006 Copyright Jody Frank

Michael Hauge is a script consultant, author and lecturer who works with writers, filmmakers and executives on their screenplays, novels, film projects and development skills. He has coached writers or consulted on projects for Warner Bros., Paramount, Disney, Columbia, New Line, Joel Silver Productions, CBS, Lifetime, Morgan Freeman, Kirsten Dunst, Robert Downey, Jr., Jennifer Lopez, Val Kilmer, and Julia Roberts.

Michael also consults with attorneys, psychologists, corporations and individuals on employing story principles in their projects, their presentations and their work with clients and patients.

Michael's book *Writing Screenplays That Sell* is a definitive reference book for the film and television industries. He is also the co-author of the very popular book for couples, *We'd Have a Great Relationship If It Weren't for You* by Dr. Bruce Derman.

Michael has presented seminars and lectures to more than 30,000 participants throughout the US, Canada and Europe, and has reached thousands more through his book, articles, CDs and DVDs. He is on the Board of Directors of the American Screenwriting Association and the Advisory Board for *ScriptWriter Magazine* in London.

He can be reached through his website at
www.ScreenplayMastery.com.

FILM & VIDEO BOOKS

Archetypes for Writers: *Using the Power of Your Subconscious*
Jennifer Van Bergen / $22.95

Art of Film Funding, The: *Alternate Financing Concepts*
Carole lee Dean / $26.95

Cinematic Storytelling: *The 100 Most Powerful Film Conventions Every Filmmaker Must Know* / Jennifer Van Sijll / $24.95

Complete Independent Movie Marketing Handbook, The: *Promote, Distribute & Sell Your Film or Video* / Mark Steven Bosko / $39.95

Creating Characters: *Let Them Whisper Their Secrets*
Marisa D'Vari / $26.95

Crime Writer's Reference Guide, The: *1001 Tips for Writing the Perfect Crime*
Martin Roth / $20.95

Cut by Cut: *Editing Your Film or Video*
Gael Chandler / $35.95

Digital Filmmaking 101, 2nd Edition: *An Essential Guide to Producing Low-Budget Movies* / Dale Newton and John Gaspard / $26.95

Directing Actors: *Creating Memorable Performances for Film and Television*
Judith Weston / $26.95

Directing Feature Films: *The Creative Collaboration Between Directors, Writers, and Actors* / Mark Travis / $26.95

Elephant Bucks: *An Insider's Guide to Writing for TV Sitcoms*
Sheldon Bull / $24.95

Eye is Quicker, The: *Film Editing; Making a Good Film Better*
Richard D. Pepperman / $27.95

Fast, Cheap & Under Control: *Lessons Learned from the Greatest Low-Budget Movies of All Time* / John Gaspard / $26.95

Fast, Cheap & Written That Way: *Top Screenwriters on Writing for Low-Budget Movies*
John Gaspard / $26.95

Film & Video Budgets, *4th Updated Edition*
Deke Simon and Michael Wiese / $26.95

Film Directing: *Cinematic Motion, 2nd Edition*
Steven D. Katz / $27.95

Film Directing: *Shot by Shot, Visualizing from Concept to Screen*
Steven D. Katz / $27.95

Film Director's Intuition, The: *Script Analysis and Rehearsal Techniques*
Judith Weston / $26.95

Film Production Management 101: *The Ultimate Guide for Film and Television Production Management and Coordination* / Deborah S. Patz / $39.95

Filmmaking for Teens: *Pulling Off Your Shorts*
Troy Lanier and Clay Nichols / $18.95

First Time Director: *How to Make Your Breakthrough Movie*
Gil Bettman / $27.95

From Word to Image: *Storyboarding and the Filmmaking Process*
Marcie Begleiter / $26.95

Hollywood Standard, The: *The Complete and Authoritative Guide to Script Format and Style* / Christopher Riley / $18.95

Independent Film Distribution: *How to Make a Successful End Run Around the Big Guys* / Phil Hall / $26.95

Independent Film and Videomakers Guide – 2nd Edition, The: *Expanded and Updated*
Michael Wiese / $29.95

Inner Drives: *How to Write and Create Characters Using the Eight Classic Centers of Motivation* / Pamela Jaye Smith / $26.95

I'll Be in My Trailer!: *The Creative Wars Between Directors & Actors*
John Badham and Craig Modderno / $26.95

Moral Premise, The: *Harnessing Virtue & Vice for Box Office Success*
Stanley D. Williams, Ph.D. / $24.95

Myth and the Movies: *Discovering the Mythic Structure of 50 Unforgettable Films*
Stuart Voytilla / $26.95

On the Edge of a Dream: *Magic and Madness in Bali*
Michael Wiese / $16.95

Perfect Pitch, The: *How to Sell Yourself and Your Movie Idea to Hollywood*
Ken Rotcop / $16.95

Power of Film, The
Howard Suber / $27.95

Psychology for Screenwriters: *Building Conflict in your Script*
William Indick, Ph.D. / $26.95

Save the Cat!: *The Last Book on Screenwriting You'll Ever Need*
Blake Snyder / $19.95

Save the Cat! Goes to the Movies: *The Screenwriter's Guide to Every Story Ever Told*
Blake Snyder / $24.95

Screenwriting 101: *The Essential Craft of Feature Film Writing*
Neill D. Hicks / $16.95

Screenwriting for Teens: *The 100 Principles of Screenwriting Every Budding Writer Must Know* / Christina Hamlett / $18.95

Script-Selling Game, The: *A Hollywood Insider's Look at Getting Your Script Sold and Produced* / Kathie Fong Yoneda / $16.95

Selling Your Story in 60 Seconds: *The Guaranteed Way to get Your Screenplay or Novel Read* / Michael Hauge / $12.95

Setting Up Your Scenes: *The Inner Workings of Great Films*
Richard D. Pepperman / $24.95

Setting Up Your Shots: *Great Camera Moves Every Filmmaker Should Know*
Jeremy Vineyard / $19.95

Shaking the Money Tree, 2nd Edition: *The Art of Getting Grants and Donations for Film and Video Projects* / Morrie Warshawski / $26.95

Sound Design: *The Expressive Power of Music, Voice, and Sound Effects in Cinema*
David Sonnenschein / $19.95

Special Effects: *How to Create a Hollywood Film Look on a Home Studio Budget* /
Michael Slone / $31.95

Stealing Fire From the Gods, 2nd Edition: *The Complete Guide to Story for Writers & Filmmakers* / James Bonnet / $26.95

Ultimate Filmmaker's Guide to Short Films, The: *Making It Big in Shorts*
Kim Adelman / $16.95

Way of Story, The: *The Craft & Soul of Writing*
Catherine Anne Jones / $22.95

Working Director, The: *How to Arrive, Thrive & Survive in the Director's Chair*
Charles Wilkinson / $22.95

Writer's Journey, – 3rd Edition, The: *Mythic Structure for Writers*
Christopher Vogler / $26.95

Writing the Action Adventure: *The Moment of Truth*
Neill D. Hicks / $14.95

Writing the Comedy Film: *Make 'Em Laugh*
Stuart Voytilla and Scott Petri / $14.95

Writing the Killer Treatment: *Selling Your Story Without a Script*
Michael Halperin / $14.95

Writing the Second Act: *Building Conflict and Tension in Your Film Script*
Michael Halperin / $19.95

Writing the Thriller Film: *The Terror Within*
Neill D. Hicks / $14.95

Writing the TV Drama Series – 2nd Edition: *How to Succeed as a Professional Writer in TV* / Pamela Douglas / $26.95

DVD & VIDEOS

Field of Fish: *VHS Video*
Directed by Steve Tanner and Michael Wiese, Written by Annamaria Murphy / $9.95

Hardware Wars: *DVD* / Written and Directed by Ernie Fosselius / $14.95

Sacred Sites of the Dalai Lamas– DVD, The: *A Pilgrimage to Oracle Lake*
A Documentary by Michael Wiese / $24.95